AMERICAN IMPERIALISM IN 1898

PROBLEMS IN AMERICAN HISTORY

EDITOR

LOREN BARITZ

State University of New York, Albany

AMERICAN IMPERIALISM IN 1898

The Quest For National Fulfillment

EDITED BY

RICHARD H. MILLER

New York University

JOHN WILEY AND SONS, INC.

New York · London · Sydney · Toronto

Library of Congress Catalogue Card Number: 71–109429

Cloth: SBN 471 60510 7   Paper: SBN 471 60511 5

Printed in the United States of America

10 9 8 7 6 5 4 3 2 1

SERIES PREFACE

This series is an introduction to the most important problems in the writing and study of American history. Some of these problems have been the subject of debate and argument for a long time, although others only recently have been recognized as controversial. However, in every case, the student will find a vital topic, an understanding of which will deepen his knowledge of social change in America.

The scholars who introduce and edit the books in this series are teaching historians who have written history in the same general area as their individual books. Many of them are leading scholars in their fields, and all have done important work in the collective search for better historical understanding.

Because of the talent and the specialized knowledge of the individual editors, a rigid editorial format has not been imposed on them. For example, some of the editors believe that primary source material is necessary to their subjects. Some believe that their material should be arranged to show conflicting interpretations. Others have decided to use the selected materials as evidence for their own interpretations. The individual editors have been given the freedom to handle their books in the way that their own experience and knowledge indicate is best. The overall result is a series built up from the individual decisions of working scholars in the various fields, rather than one that conforms to a uniform editorial decision.

A common goal (rather than a shared technique) is the bridge of this series. There is always the desire to bring the reader as close to these problems as possible. One result of this objective is an emphasis of the nature and consequences of problems and events, with a de-emphasis of the more purely historiographical issues. The goal is to involve the student in the reality of crisis, the inevitability of ambiguity, and the excitement of finding a way through the historical maze.

Above all, this series is designed to show students how experienced historians read and reason. Although health is not contagious, intellectual engagement may be. If we show students something significant in a phrase or a passage that they otherwise may have missed, we will have accomplished part of our objective. When students see something that passed us by, then the process will have been made whole. This active and mutual involvement of editor and reader with a significant human problem will rescue the study of history from the smell and feel of dust.

Loren Baritz

ACKNOWLEDGEMENTS

Every book, whatever its significance, represents a collective effort, from intellectual instigation through production and publication. While absolving them from any errors or *lacunae* contained herein, sincere thanks are due to several people who helped make this a better book than it might otherwise have been. Jules Davids, Norman A. Graebner, David F. Healy, Julius W. Pratt and William A. Williams provided constructive criticism concerning my thinking on the nature and development of American imperialism. Loren Baritz and William L. Gum were instrumental in launching the project, even to the extent of deciding upon a proper title. Robert A. Divine and David M. Reimers gave the manuscript a thorough reading, providing additional insights and raising new issues. Keith Nave and Joan Rosenberg were most pleasant and patient, competent and cooperative in superintending the production of the book. Finally, a note of appreciation for the high tolerance level of the other three members of a 'fun' family.

Washington, D.C.

R.H.M.

CONTENTS

AMERICAN IMPERIALISM IN 1898

INTRODUCTION

It has long been a historical—and historians'—maxim that each generation writes its own history. One of the prime exceptions to this unwritten rule over the years was the study of the genesis and continuity of American expansion, both continental and overseas. But, during the past generation, it has been something of a psychic Lorelei for many historians who have attempted to analyze this aspect of America's past. Prior to 1945 most of the studies on this subject shared a common propensity for self-righteous chauvinism, in which America was portrayed as something akin to a Divine Instrument in the pursuit of its expansionist destiny at the expense of the lesser worthies of God's creation, be they Indians, Frenchmen, Tories, Spaniards or Mexicans.

Such a parochial outlook was bound to create new difficulties when the United States embarked upon a new era of expansion beyond her continental confines. Because she had succumbed, as Richard W. Van Alstyne has noted, to the self-imposed myth that "in the United States, it is almost a heresy to describe the nation as an empire," it was incumbent upon both partisan polemicists and dispassionate historians to rationalize the dramatic events of 1898, the year in which American overseas ambitions fully crystallized. Both elements tended to view this imperial thrust as a single-dimensional phenomenon precipitated by the Spanish-American War, but each subscribed to differing interpretations in explaining the dynamics of motivation.

Representative of the former category was the contemporary effort of Henry Cabot Lodge, the self-proclaimed "scholar in politics" of his time, until the title was pre-empted by Woodrow Wilson. Like most other "inside" histories, Lodge's *The War*

1

With Spain, published in 1899, was victimized by its very inti-
macy with the problems and suffered in varying degrees from a
lack of perspective, detachment, and accuracy. For the Massachusetts Senator and ostensible co-leader of the "large policy"
clique of American expansionists, the war with Spain and its
"beneficial" consequences demonstrated that Divine Providence
was still on the side of the American angels. In an ethereal-like
prose style he defended the American demand for the entire
Philippine archipelago, chanting: "The American commissioners
heard in all this, as the great master of music heard in the first
bars of his immortal symphony 'the hand of fate knocking at
the door.' Some of them had always believed in the outcome,
some had not, but all became absolutely convinced that there
was but one road possible. . . ."

Conversely, most of the professional scholars who studied the
subject were content with Americanizing Sir John Seeley's famous
aphorism that the British Empire had been created during a
state of absence of mind. Thus evolved the "great aberration"
thesis, which attempted to explain American actions in the
1890's as a product of some form of collective irrational activism.
Central to this hypothesis was the contention that the events
of 1898 marked a commencement, rather than a culmination,
of American policy. Even the Almighty was taken to task as a
guilty accessory as historians recounted at face value the interview between President McKinley and a group of Methodist
ministers (published in the New York *Christian Advocate* on
22 January 1903, more than sixteen months after McKinley had
been hastened to his grave by the pistol of Leon Czolgosz). In
this interview, McKinley ostensibly confessed that "the truth is
I didn't want the Philippines and when they came to us as a
gift from the gods, I did not know what to do about them. . . . I
sought counsel from all sides—Democrats as well as Republicans—
but got little help." But, following prayerful consultation with
his Maker, he decided that "there was nothing left for us to do
but to take them all and to educate the Filipinos, and uplift
and civilize and Christianize them, and by God's grace do the
very best we could by them as our fellow-men for whom Christ
also died." The rhetoric may have impressed his Protestant

listeners, but it conveniently ignored the Spanish Catholic presence in those islands during the previous four centuries; it also withheld much of the basic information that contributed to the policy decision resulting in total annexation.

However, this older approach has been altered drastically in the years since 1945 because of two dominant factors: viz., the unearthing of new significant evidence and a new environmental ethos in which present-day historians have been forced to write. America's active participation in the Hundred Years' War of the twentieth century (more commonly referred to at this time as World War I, World War II, and the so-called Cold War) has brought in its wake global responsibilities and has further added to the distressing complexity of examining the past in light of current events. This was especially true in the months and years following the surrender of Germany and Japan, because the United States was confronted by a cruel dilemma, the consequences of which will have an impact on American foreign policy for decades to come. In Europe the destruction of the Nazi regime created a geopolitical power void of such apparent dimensions that the continent seemed ripe for conquest on the part of an aggressive, expansionist Soviet colossus. The one response deemed most appropriate was the revivification of the war-wracked western "democracies" so as to "contain" the Communist challenge from the East. Paradoxically, this approach also seemed to imply the reconstitution of their tottering empires in the third world, where the forces of nascent nationalism and anticolonialism combined with a common hatred of the occidental aesthetic and material value system to produce a new era of conflict. In addition, the frustration of nonproductive American military involvements in Korea, Laos, and Vietnam have only served to intensify the search for a fuller understanding of our past performances in the realm of overseas expansion.

Contrary to the conventional wisdom and the literary assaults of the disaffected Right, the impetus for a scholarly re-examination of this subject did not emanate from the so-called "New Left" among the younger generation of American historians. Nor did it evolve from the so-called Wisconsin school of American Diplomatic History, that group of scholars at Madison led by

Fred Harvey Harrington and William A. Williams and those
who studied with them. (Ostensibly, this group is said to adhere
to an *a priori*, neo-Beardian economic determinist, neo-isolation-
ist philosophy in their analysis of the American expansionist
past.) Ironically, the first step toward a more candid re-examination of the problem came in August of 1949 (Williams was then
still in the process of finishing his graduate studies under
Harrington), when the State Department published its famous
White Paper on American relations with China during the
preceding half-century. In an effort to absolve the Roosevelt
and Truman Administrations from the jingo charges, by Senator
Joseph McCarthy and the "Formosa Lobby," that the State
Department and its presidential overlords had been criminally
responsible for the catastrophe that had befallen the Kuomintang
regime of Chiang Kai-Shek, the documents dealt primarily with
the period 1944–1949. However, the documentation for the
earlier period implied an admission of governmental bureau-
cratic inadequacy in developing a proper relationship between
policy ends and means in the promotion of the twin goals of
the Open Door (read equal economic exploitation for all the
Occidental powers?) and the territorial integrity of China. This
official acknowledgment of diplomatic defeat paved the way for
serious reconsiderations of America's expansionist past, based
not on the presumption of national self-righteousness, but on a
meticulous examination of all the evidence, old and new, both
at home and abroad. The result has been a more soul-searching
and less self-laudatory reassessment of past realities and, hope-
fully, a better appreciation and understanding of the complexity
of present and future overseas involvements.

For both present-day historians and their counterparts of
earlier generations, the fundamental argument has been the
attempt to establish—or disprove—the continuity of cause-and-
effect relationships in the history of American expansionism.
Almost without exception, historians are now willing to accept
the notion that there was a certain consistency in our continental
outlook, regardless of party, sectional, or economic affiliation.
Whether it was Thomas Jefferson envisioning an "empire for
liberty," or John Quincy Adams advocating the Monroe Doctrine

as an ideological weapon for thwarting Tsarist expansion, or Whig merchants dreaming of an "Empire On The Pacific," the common denominator for each was the conception of America as a continental colossus, unchallenged by the powers of Europe, or by weak neighbors to the north and south. During this era of "free security," as C. Vann Woodward has labeled it, the country was able to determine its own pace of expansion, unharried by foreign foes and having the luxury of time to cope with such internal vicissitudes as the furor engendered by the slave controversy and the extension of the "peculiar institution" into the territories acquired by purchase from France, by extortion from Spain, and by conquest from Mexico.

By the time of the Civil War, the United States had determined the skeletal outlines of its continental domains, and had developed an ideology of expansion by which it could bridge the gap between its domestic achievements and its unfulfilled overseas ambitions. Those ambitions were not developed in the decade of the 1890's, nor were they transposed from theory to fact by the so-called "psychic crisis" set in motion by the depression of 1893. Quite the contrary, for it must be recalled that serious American interest in the acquisition of Cuba and Santo Domingo can be traced back to the days of the Jefferson Administration, while the writings of John Quincy Adams and the Clayton-Bulwer treaty clearly demonstrated our early and continued interest in the American development of an isthmian canal. Likewise, in the Pacific, the desire to acquire the Hawaiian Islands certainly antedated the Civil War.

It was William H. Seward who, as Secretary of State during the Lincoln and Johnson Administrations, coalesced the fragmented approaches of his predecessors into an expansionist master plan. Seward's scheme envisioned an integrated empire that would be developed along carefully programmed lines, beginning with a strong continental base (including Canada and Latin America), and moving systematically from an insular network in the Caribbean across the way stations of the Pacific, by means of an isthmian canal and Hawaii, toward the ultimate goal of Asia. In the ensuing two decades Secretaries of State Fish, Evarts, and even Frelinghuysen labored in various ways to achieve Seward's master plan, albeit without any significant success. Working along parallel lines (if not always in conjunction with the intellectuals, the military strategists, and those elements of the business community who viewed foreign markets as vitally important for their economic welfare), State Department policy by the 1890's, whether in the hands of Blaine, Gresham or Olney, seemed consciously devoted to the furtherance of these expansionist goals, despite the domestic pressures exerted in the form of agrarian agitation and the aforementioned depression of 1893. Thus, whether it was due to ideological reasons as espoused in the concept of Manifest Destiny or its several variants (Darwinist ethics, a "psychic crisis," or the lust for overseas markets), one fact clearly emerged; viz., that by 1890, the United States was politically, socially, and economically prepared to accept the blessings—and burdens—of imperialism. All that was wanting was the proper time and circumstance, that favorable opportunity usually (and improperly) described as an accident of history.

Seen in this context, the unending Cuban resistance to Spanish colonialism, which flared anew into open rebellion in 1895, provided such a favorable opportunity for American intervention, either in the form of diplomatic coercion or in the ultimate recourse to formal hostilities against Spain. Both alternatives were given serious contingency planning by the Cleveland Administration (for instance, in December of 1896 Lieutenant William W. Kimball of the Office of Naval Intelligence was ordered to draft battle plans for an American assault on the Spanish base at Manila), despite its professed stance of formal neutrality and the nonrecognition of Cuban belligerency. The episode of the de Lôme letter (an indiscreet personal attack on McKinley by the Spanish Minister in Washington, which was pilfered by a Cuban agent and published in the Hearst papers on 9 February 1898), and the sinking of the second-class battleship U.S.S. Maine in Havana harbor six days later thus were not causes of, but contributing factors to, a war with Spain. In all likelihood, the war was made inevitable by a combination of factors: Spanish sloth and/or refusal in initiating internal reforms in Cuba, even under duress; a congenital American inability to understand the Spanish life-style, especially as it was displayed in time of crisis; and McKinley's failure to achieve his expansionist aims by coercive diplomacy.

In years past it was also fashionable to argue that yellow journalism had played a prominent part in promoting hostilities. One such historian, Joseph E. Wisan, even went so far as to proclaim that "the Spanish-American War would not have occurred had not the appearance of Hearst in New York journalism precipitated a bitter battle for newspaper circulation." Despite this assertion, more recent scholarship has reduced drastically the dimensions of the war-hawk roles played by Hearst, Pulitzer, and the other jingo journalists of the period.

But one unresolved problem which is still a matter of historical contention is the role played by the business community in the advent of the war with Spain. Until the appearance in 1936 of Julius W. Pratt's *Expansionists Of 1898,* most historians were prone to perpetuate the theory that "Big Business" had propelled the McKinley Administration down the road to war. Pratt's central thesis that "the rise of an expansionist philosophy in the United States owed little to economic influences" and "business interests . . . were generally opposed to expansion, or indifferent to it, until after May 1, 1898," and the evidence he cited to sustain it, seemingly reversed overnight the trend of interpretation; it even converted such a renowned economic determinist as Harold U. Faulkner. Coincidentally, Pratt's book also had a contemporary relevance, in that it was used as an indirect rebuttal to the sensational disclosures forthcoming at that time (1934–1936) from the Special Senate Committee Investigating The Munitions Industry, better known as the Nye Committee. This committee, headed by Senator Gerald P. Nye, a Progressive Republican from North Dakota, had uncovered definite links between the arms makers in this country and the politicians abroad, especially during the periods of the first World War and the aftermath of Versailles. Moreover, Nye had gone so far as to claim that Wilson had deliberately lied to the people concerning America's supposed neutrality and Wilson's presumed nonknowledge of the secret Allied treaties negotiated prior to American entry in 1917. Although Pratt's book served as a temporary deterrent, it did not stop the flow of criticism concerning the close working relationship between the business community and belligerent governments in war-climate situations, nor did it prevent the further flow of revisionist studies such as that of Charles C. Tansill and others on the (im)morality of Wilsonian diplomacy.

A new challenge to the Pratt thesis was raised in the decade of the 1960s by William A. Williams, Walter LaFeber, and others who examined the role of business in the months before the declaration of war with Spain. Their arguments that the business community, in its search for new markets and an expansion of the Open Door, willingly supported a hard-line Administration policy, even if it meant war, gained increased currency in an age in which the "military-industrial complex" (a term made famous by Dwight D. Eisenhower, one of the best friends each component ever had) was under constant attack by the press, the public, the intellectuals, and even a sizeable minority of the Congress. In retrospect, it would seem that, in 1898, as in any other period of American history before the rise of corporate conglomerates, the attitude of the business community could not be deemed monolithic in its support for, or opposition to, the war against Spain. Those corporations with vested interests in Cuba, and those who expected to profit from the issuance of lucrative war contracts or benefit from overseas acquisitions, obviously were more concerned than their noninvolved counterparts in the industrial and commercial arena. Until further evidence is forthcoming from the files of business organizations and their leaders during this period, it would seem that there is merit to both arguments, since each has examined the activities of only a portion of the overall business community.

The historiographical heat generated in assessing the origins of the war with Spain is nothing when compared with the conflicting interpretations that have evolved concerning its consequences. At the outset it must be admitted that Clausewitz's dictum that war is the extension of diplomacy by other means was never more true than in this instance. There is little doubt that the outbreak of hostilities expedited the annexation of Hawaii, though McKinley still took the cautious route in presenting the matter to Congress as a Joint Resolution, which required a simple majority vote in each House, rather than having recourse to the more orthodox treaty process that might have risked a third defeat by the Senate, the previous two attempts having failed to gain the requisite two-thirds majority. There was a presidential precedent for such action. Back in 1844 a proposed treaty for the annexation of Texas had been decisively defeated by the Senate. However, following the presidential election of that year, in which James K. Polk emerged as a narrow victor over Henry Clay, many felt that the results represented something of a mandate on the Texas question. One such believer was the lame-duck President, John Tyler, who, in the waning days of his Administration, presided over the annexation of Texas (more than a year prior to the outbreak of war with Mexico) by Congressional Joint Resolution. On such tenuous grounds are presidential precedents established, wars precipitated, and empires expanded.

On the other hand, the more one studies the nature of the American involvement in Cuba during this period, the more one suspects that the only aberration in our policy regarding the "Pearl of the Antilles" was the Congressional decision to approve the Teller Amendment as a qualifying factor in the American declaration of war. This self-denying ordinance, which deprived us of possession rights in advance of the island's expected conquest, seems to have surprised the McKinley Administration and restricted its diplomatic options, not only in terms of further coercive action short of war, but also with respect to a more favorable armistice and peace settlement. Accordingly, one might then infer that the acquisition of Puerto Rico was something in the nature of a consolation prize. But until more substantive evidence is available, such speculation must remain confined to the realm of scholarly conjecture.

Of course, the greatest controversy centers over the American involvement in the Philippines, militarily, diplomatically, and politically. The records of the Navy Department reveal, and the memoirs of George Dewey confirm, that as early as 1873, the United States contemplated an attack upon the Spanish base at Manila. As noted above, this idea was revived and contingency battle plans were ordered drawn up in the waning months of the second Cleveland Administration. Following the destruction of the *Maine,* the Philippines assumed a prominent role in Administration thinking. Contrary to the long-accepted view that Theodore Roosevelt was primarily responsible for preparing Dewey's dramatic descent upon Manilla, the documents clearly indicate that similar and more comprehensive orders had been sent to Dewey at the behest of McKinley a week prior to Roosevelt's famous cable of 25 February 1898. In addition, the papers of John Bassett Moore, then serving as Assistant Secretary of State and charged with the task of drawing up a draft peace settlement following Dewey's victory at Manila Bay, offer further revealing insights into Roosevelt's thinking at this time. As late as 9 May, more than a week after the Administration learned of Dewey's defeat of the Spanish fleet, Roosevelt, upon hearing of Moore's orders, personally visited him and "specially warned" him "against the acquisition of the Philippines" which lay "far beyond" what Roosevelt considered to be the proper perimeters of American governmental control. Other recent studies, such as that of William E. Livezey on Alfred Thayer Mahan (who felt that the Philippines might be missed by the United States no more than a "joint of a little finger") and the essays of J. A. S. Grenville and George B. Young on Henry Cabot Lodge, indicate that the influence of the "large policy" advocates in promoting and effecting America's decision to "go imperial" has been vastly overrated.

Two other salient points of controversy with respect to the annexation of the Philippines are the roles respectively played by President McKinley and William Jennings Bryan, perennial presidential hopeful and the titular leader of the Democratic Party at this juncture. Older interpretations of McKinley subscribed to the notion that he was a weak and vacillating man in a time of crisis. They reflected Roosevelt's fulmination that McKinley had "no more backbone than a chocolate eclair." A contemporary joke of the period ran: "Q. Why is McKinley's mind like a hotel bed? A. Because it has to be made up for him before he can use it." However, recent scholarship has shown that, even though McKinley may have been sadly underestimated by many historians, such was not the case with the power brokers of the time, both in and out of Congress. His careful selection of the peace delegation and the solicitous nurturing of public opinion in marshaling support for annexation decisions long since taken indicate that here was an adroit political tactician who, in some respects, possessed almost Byzantine qualities in the circuitous pursuit of his policy aims.

Conversely, the myth of Bryan's overriding influence in switching Senate votes from opposition to support of the Peace of Paris has been exploded by recent researches. For many years historians relied exclusively on the memoir account of Senator George F. Hoar (R-Mass.) that Bryan single-handedly persuaded seventeen members of the upper chamber to change their votes on a peace treaty that included total annexation of the Philippines. At the same time these historians dismissed as invalid a memoir account entitled *Imperial Washington*, written by Senator Richard F. Pettigrew, a maverick Republican from South Dakota who had bolted the party in 1896 to support Bryan. Pettigrew, whose reputation for honesty in presenting issues was something less than adequate, claimed that Bryan had not been able to influence a single vote in either direction, because he had nothing to offer except promises, whereas the agents of the McKinley Administration were able to "deliver" with federal judgeships, postmasterships, and outright bribes, as the occasion warranted.

The final Senate vote on the treaty, taken on the afternoon of 6 February 1899, came within hours of the receipt of the news of a Filipino insurrection against American control in the islands. The apparent closeness of the final tally, 57 to 27, one vote in excess of the required two-thirds majority, did not tell the entire story. For example, subsequent examination of the documents now available indicate that Senator Lodge had an additional four votes to call upon, if such a recourse had proved necessary. Moreover, if the pre-vote estimate had indicated the nonacceptance of the treaty, McKinley would certainly have withdrawn it from Senate consideration and awaited the arrival of the 56th Congress, which was due to convene on 4 March 1899. This forthcoming Congress contained, among others, eight new Senators pledged to the Presidential program of expansion. All of them had defeated antiexpansion incumbents in the Congressional elections of 1898. (It must be remembered that, in those days prior to the passage of the Seventeenth Amendment, Senators were not elected by popular vote but by the State legislatures, which were then much more responsive to partisan dictates from Washington).

In the final analysis, it is somewhat ironic that the assertion of Pettigrew was vindicated over that of Hoar as a result of the efforts of subsequent scholars, such as Paolo E. Coletta, who demonstrated the complete futility of Bryan's role in the treaty fight. Here was a confused idealist who, as Paxton Hibben wryly commented, viewed the Spanish-American War as "a game to be won by sacrifice hits." A lifelong pacifist, he volunteered for military service, only to wind up battling a siege of dysentery in a disease-infested army camp near Jacksonville, Florida. Ardently opposed to imperialism in any form, he nonetheless supported the treaty of peace on the premise that the Republicans would be saddled with the onus of its consequences in the Presidential election of 1900. The Republicans joyfully accepted this burden and used it to defeat the quixotic "Great Commoner" in 1900 even more decisively than they had in 1896.

The continuance of American military involvements in the period of the Cold War has generated renewed interest in the activities of the anti-imperialists of 1898. Like their expansionist counterparts, the anti-imperialists also appealed to the loftier aspects of the American past, denouncing overseas imperialism as a denial of that democracy fostered by the Founding Fathers. Paradoxically, both sides employed racist arguments to substantiate their respective positions. Such a man as Senator John T. Morgan of Alabama advocated the annexation of both Cuba and the Philippines because he envisioned them as the final solution of the "nigger problem"; viz., insular depots for the relocation of the black minorities in the United States. In opposition, Senator "Pitchfork Ben" Tillman of South Carolina opposed overseas acquisitions for fear that they would further mongrelize and contaminate the white population on the mainland, while creating new hope for social and political advancement for the black minorities at home. Many Northerners, whether *pro* or *con* on the imperial issue, argued in the same vein, but utilized more pseudoscientific or proto-Darwinian rationales for their respective positions. But, as Christopher Lasch has observed, they shared a common basic assumption in that "they accepted the inequality of man—or, to be more precise, of races—as an established fact of life."

However, many of the contemporary writers on the subject (regardless of which position they espoused in their analyses) have been mesmerized by the American involvement in Vietnam. Insensitive to the historian's self-imposed *caveat* that historical time and circumstance are seldom, if ever, twice the same, they have been prone to draw analogies between the anti-imperialists of 1898 and those of the present era that are not warranted by the available evidence. There is still much work to be done on the historical role of pacificism and antiwar movements in our previous history before we can begin to formulate any broad-based hypotheses on the subject.

The consequences of such an activist program of expansionism in 1898 have had global repercussions, both for the United States and its counterparts in the big leagues of power politics. America's formal entrance into the imperial arena forced it to play the game according to the rules established by those contestants already in the fray. Thus the Open Door policy, contrary to accepted historical traditions, did not suddenly emerge as some new Presidential policy in the years 1899–1900. As Tyler Dennett long ago noted, the Open Door policy as a conscious *modus operandi* in American overseas activity was as old as the Declaration of Independence; the only reason why the task had gone so long unfinished in Asia before 1898 "was merely that the American people had not cared enough about the markets of Asia to finish it." McKinley, in his instructions to the Peace Commissioners before sending them off to Paris, reminded them that the Open Door was already a long-standing pillar of American policy, and could not be compromised in any fashion by the defeated Spanish.

Viewed in this context, the issuance of the Hay notes in the months following the Peace of Paris were little more than the adaptation of a vintage policy to the realities of the then current situation in East Asia. In return, Hay secretly hoped to obtain a territorial foothold on the mainland of Asia by acquiring a naval station at Samsah Bay in Fukien province. However, given the stress Hay had placed in these notes on Chinese territorial integrity and the Sino-Japanese nonalienation agreement on Fukien (which would have entailed prior, and unlikely, Japanese approval of any American acquisition in that area), the proposal seemed to be a self-defeating one. In the same vein, as Raymond A. Esthus has shown, the United States, in succeeding Presidential administrations continued to adjust to the changing power balances on the mainland of Asia. Hay's failure in promoting the Open Door for trade but not for investment redounded to American disadvantage; by the time of the Lansing-Ishii agreement of 1917, the United States was on the diplomatic defensive, in China and East Asia, both politically and economically.

However, the failure to expand the scope of the Open Door in China did not deter the United States from continuing its expansionist activities elsewhere in the world during the twentieth century. Although failure marked the government's efforts to obtain a naval base at Samsah Bay, it did acquire extended possession rights for naval installations in such places as Guantánamo Bay in Cuba, the Canal Zone in Panama, Subig Bay in the Philippines, and Camranh Bay in South Vietnam, bases which were retained long after these areas had been promised or granted their independence. In addition, although the government and its people came to reject the notion of formal empire as a means of maintaining American influence abroad, it persisted in pursuing the quest for informal empire, continually in Latin America and, after 1945, in Asia. This was accomplished by the twin techniques of either, or some combination of both, strategic economic assistance (either in the form of private investments or official government "foreign aid" programs, more often than not in the form of military hardware) and selective U.S. military intervention in order to maintain a predominant American presence against the challenges of real or imagined adversaries in a particular area of activity. Whether there will be any surcease of, or increase in, such activity in the future, in the wake of the domestic and diplomatic consequences accruing from recent activities of this sort, is still a matter of conjecture.

To examine the mood, mode, and mechanics of American overseas expansion at the end of the nineteenth century is to open a Pandora's box of intriguing dimensions. There can be no doubt that a proper understanding of this aspect of America's past is absolutely necessary for anyone who would seek to comprehend the complexities of American involvement in the world arena in the present century. For these reasons I have chosen to focus almost exclusively on the events of 1898 so as to demonstrate the meaningful interaction between the deep-moving forces of historical change and the so-called accidents of history that were the midwives of such a dramatic and, on occasion, traumatic, catharsis. The selections that follow, whether primary source documents or secondary source excerpts, have been designed to elaborate many of the arguments made in this essay, or to counter some of those hypotheses herein presented that are still a source of serious historical debate.

The headnotes that introduce each selection should be read with care, since they raise issues that the reader ought to resolve for himself, on the basis of the evidence presented. In addition, he should also pay close attention to the background information presented on each of the secondary writers. Carl Becker's dictum that "everyman [is] his own historian" must be qualified by the self-realization that every historian's outlook on the past about which he has written has been influenced to some extent by his own family, ethnic, religious, educational and social background. Thus a new theorem might adjure all interested in history, before reading any study of the past, to learn something about the historian who wrote it. In a world of fallible men, there is no such thing as "objective" history. The best one can hope for is an honest attempt on the part of all to conceptualize past reality and present it in comprehensive—and comprehensible—fashion to those present and future readers searching for a better understanding of the world as they apprehend it. This is especially true with respect to an examination of the historical implications of 1898, because upon a proper awareness and appreciation of their significance and consequences may rest the ultimate destiny of the United States.

Rudyard Kipling
The White Man's Burden

(The United States and the Philippine Islands)
Take up the White Man's burden—
  Send forth the best ye breed—
Go bind your sons to exile
  To serve your captives' need;
To wait in heavy harness
  On fluttered folk and wild—
Your new-caught, sullen peoples,
  Half devil and half child.

Take up the White Man's burden—
  In patience to abide,
To veil the threat of terror
  And check the show of pride;
By open speech and simple,
  An hundred times made plain,
To seek another's profit,
  And work another's gain.

Take up the White Man's burden—
  The savage wars of peace—
Fill full the mouth of Famine
  And bid the sickness cease;
And when your goal is nearest
  The end for others sought,
Watch Sloth and heathen Folly
  Bring all your hope to nought.

Take up the White Man's burden—
  No tawdry rule of kings,
But toil of serf and sweeper—
  The tale of common things.

SOURCE. Rudyard Kipling, "The White Man's Burden," from *The Five Nations*, by Rudyard Kipling. Reprinted by permission of Mrs. George Bambridge, Doubleday & Company, Inc., and the Macmillan Company.

The ports ye shall not enter,
 The roads ye shall not tread,
Go make them with your living,
 And mark them with your dead!

Take up the White Man's burden—
 And reap his old reward:
The blame of those ye better,
 The hate of those ye guard—
The cry of hosts ye humour
 (Ah, slowly!) toward the light:—
"Why brought ye us from bondage,
 "Our loved Egyptian night?"

Take up the White Man's burden—
 Ye dare not stoop to less—
Nor call too loud on Freedom
 To cloak your weariness;
By all ye cry or whisper,
 By all ye leave or do,
The silent, sullen peoples
 Shally weight your Gods and you.

Take up the White Man's burden—
 Have done with childish days—
The lightly proffered laurels,
 The easy, ungrudged praise.
Comes now, to search your manhood
 Through all the thankless years,
Cold-edged with dear-bought wisdom
 The judgment of your peers!

PART ONE

The Rationales for American Overseas Expansion

THE RATIONALES FOR
AMERICAN OVERSEAS EXPANSION

1   *Julius W. Pratt*

It Was au Courant *Manifest Destiny*

Educated at Davidson College and the University of Chicago (Ph.D., 1924), Julius W. Pratt (1888–   ), professor emeritus at the State University at Buffalo and the University of Notre Dame, has long been recognized as one of the foremost students on the history of American expansionism. His published books on the subject include Expansionists of 1812, Expansionists of 1898, and America's Colonial Experiment. In this essay, as in his other publications, Pratt has sought to demonstrate the continuity of the ideology of "Manifest Destiny" in the American expansionist tradition. Despite the changing currents of time and circumstance, note that the principal common denominator in each instance was an appeal to the Deity to sanction what had been done—or was about to be done. What reaction does this type of self-righteous moralism elicit in a contemporary society whose attitudes are becoming increasingly secularized?

Lincoln Steffens has observed that Americans have never learned to do wrong knowingly; that whenever they compromise with principle or abandon it, they invariably find a pious justification

SOURCE. Julius W. Pratt, "The Ideology of American Expansion," in Avery O. Craven, ed., *Essays in Honor of William E. Dodd,* copyright 1935 by the University of Chicago Press, pp. 335–353. Reprinted by permission of the publisher and the author.

for their action. One is reminded of this observation in reviewing the history of American territorial expansion. For every
step in that process, ingenious minds have found the best of
reasons. From the year 1620, when King James the First granted
to the Council for New England certain "large and goodlye
Territoryes" in order "to second and followe God's sacred Will,"
to the year 1898, when William McKinley alleged that he had
divine sanction for taking the Philippine Islands, it has been
found possible to fit each successive acquisition of territory into
the pattern of things decreed by divine will or inescapable
destiny. The avowal of need or greed, coupled with power to
take, has never satisfied our national conscience. We needed
Florida and the mouth of the Mississippi; we thought we needed
Canada, Texas, Oregon, California. But when we took, or attempted to take, that which we needed, we persuaded ourselves
that we were but fulfilling the designs of Providence or the laws
of Nature. If some of the apologists for later ventures in expansion were more frank in avowing motives of "national
interest," the pious or fatalistic justification was none the less
present.

The idea of a destiny which presides over and guides American
expansion has rarely, if ever, been absent from the national consciousness. The precise character of that destiny, however, as
well as the ultimate goal to which it points, have varied with
changing ideas and circumstances. One of its earliest forms was
geographical determinism. Certain contiguous areas were thought
of as surely destined for annexation because their location made
them naturally part of the United States. . . .

What were the "natural boundaries" of the young republic?
One mode of determining them was defined by Jefferson. Writing to Madison in 1809 of the hope of acquiring Cuba, he said:
"Cuba can be defended by us without a navy, and this develops
the principle which ought to limit our views. Nothing should
ever be accepted which would require a navy to defend it."
Northwardly, Jefferson visioned Canada as eventually to be
drawn under the American flag; southwardly, Florida, Cuba, and
probably Texas. On the west he apparently thought of the
Rocky Mountains as forming the natural boundary. The West

Coast would be peopled "with free and independent Americans, unconnected with us but by the ties of blood and interest, and employing like us the rights of self-government." Sheer distance seemed an insuperable barrier to the incorporation of the Oregon country in the American Union. . . .

Such restricted ideas of the nation's natural boundaries were not to survive for many years. . . . It was inevitable that the coming of the railroad and, later, of the telegraph should result in an expanding conception of the nation's natural boundaries. Daniel Webster could still maintain in 1845 that there would arise an independent "Pacific republic" on the west coast, but for many others the "throne of Terminus" had moved on from the Rockies to the shores of the Pacific. The *Democratic Review*, leading organ of the expansionists of the Mexican War era, predicted in 1845 that a railroad to the Pacific would soon be a reality, and that "the day cannot be far distant which shall witness the conveyance of the representatives from Oregon and California to Washington within less time than a few years ago was devoted to a similar journey by those from Ohio." The telegraph, furthermore, would soon enable Pacific coast newspapers "to set up in type the first half of the President's Inaugural, before the echoes of the latter half shall have died away beneath the lofty porch of the Capitol, as spoken from his lips." In the debate on the Oregon question in the House of Representatives in January, 1846, the significance of the Pacific as a natural boundary was repeatedly stressed. From the Atlantic to the Pacific, said Bowlin of Missouri, "we were by nature, ay, we were stamped by the hand of God himself, as one nation of men." Similarly, in the debate of 1844 and 1845 over the annexation of Texas, the Rio Grande with the neighboring strips of desert country had been portrayed as the divinely fixed natural boundary of the United States on the southwest.

If a divine hand had shaped the outlines of the North American continent with a view to its attaining political unity, the divine mind was thought to be by no means indifferent to the type of political organism which should dominate it. The American god of the early nineteenth century was the God of Democracy, and his followers had no doubt that he had reserved the continent for a democratic nation. Jefferson may not have regarded this consummation as a divinely appointed destiny, but he certainly contemplated as probable and desirable the spread of democratic institutions throughout the continent. The true flowering of this idea, however, belongs properly to the Jacksonian era, and its most enthusiastic exponent was the *Democratic Review,* a monthly magazine founded and for many years edited by Mr. John L. O'Sullivan. This exuberant Irish-American, whose faith in the institutions of his adopted country was irrepressible, not only coined the phrase "manifest destiny" but for years expounded in the pages of the *Review* the idea which it embodied.

The *Democratic Review* was founded in 1837. In the issue for November, 1839, appeared an article, presumably by O'Sullivan entitled "The Great Nation of Futurity." This role was to be America's it was argued,

"because the principle upon which a nation is organized fixes its destiny, and that of equality is perfect, is universal. . . . Besides, the truthful annals of any nation furnish abundant evidence that its happiness, its greatness, its duration, were always proportionate to the democratic equality in its system of government. . . . We point to the everlasting truth on the first page of our national declaration, and we proclaim to the millions of other lands, that 'the gates of hell'—the powers of aristocracy and monarchy—'shall not prevail against it'."

Thus happily founded upon the perfect principle of equality, the United States was destined to a unique success. Her shining example should "smite unto death the tyranny of kings, hierarchs, and oligarchs." What all this portended for the future boundaries of the United States the writer did not state except in poetic language. "Its floor shall be a hemisphere," he wrote, "its roof the firmament of the star studded heavens, and its congregation an Union of many Republics, comprising hundreds of happy millions, ... governed by God's natural and moral law of equality. . . . ." Within a few years, however, the *Democratic Review* became sufficiently concrete in its ideas of the extent of the democratizing mission of the United States. Texas, Oregon, California, Canada, and much or all of Mexico, were to receive the blessings of American principles. The American continent had been reserved by Providence for the dawn of a new era, when men should be ready to throw off the antique systems of Europe and live in the light of equality and reason. The time was now at hand, and no American should shrink from the task of spreading the principles of liberty over all the continent. Cuba, too, had been left by Providence in the hands of a weak power until the United States was ready for it. Now it, like the rest, was "about to be annexed to the model republic." . . .

Neither natural boundaries nor divinely favored institutions were in themselves sufficient to insure the peopling of the continent by the favored race. The third essential factor was seen in what more than one Congressman termed "the American multiplication table." "Go to the West," said Kennedy of Indiana in 1846, "and see a young man with his mate of eighteen; after the lapse of thirty years, visit him again and and instead of two, you will find twenty-two. This is what I call the American multiplication table." Apparently Jefferson had in mind this same fecundity of the Anglo-Saxon race in America when he predicted in 1786 that "our confederacy must be viewed as the nest from which all America, North & South is to be peopled," and when in 1803 he expressed full confidence in the growth of such an American population on the Mississippi "as will be able to do their own business" in securing control of New Orleans. On the same principle, Barbour of Virginia foretold in 1825 the peopling of the Oregon country by Americans.

It was partly, too, upon the basis of this unexampled growth in numbers that the editor of the *Democratic Review* founded his doctrine of "manifest destiny." It was in an unsigned article in the number for July-August, 1845, that the phrase first appeared. The writer charged foreign nations with attempting to impede the annexation of Texas, with the object of "checking the fulfillment of our manifest destiny to overspread the continent allotted by Providence for the free development of our yearly multiplying millions." Texas, he said, had been

"absorbed into the Union in the inevitable fulfilment of the general law which is rolling our population westward; the connexion of which with that ratio of growth in population which is destined within a hundred years to swell our numbers to the enormous population of *two hundred and fifty millions* (if not more), is too evident to leave us in doubt of the manifest design of Providence in regard to the occupation of this continent."

When war with Mexico came, and the more rabid expansionists were seeking excuses for annexing large portions of Mexican territory, a different side of the idea of racial superiority was advanced. The Mexicans, it seemed, had a destiny too—how different from that of their northern neighbors! "The Mexican race," said the *Democratic Review,* "now see, in the fate of the aborigines of the north, their own inevitable destiny. They must amalgamate and be lost, in the superior vigor of the Anglo-Saxon race, or they must utterly perish." *The New York Evening Post* indorsed the idea, sanctifying it in the name of Providence. "Providence has so ordained it; and it is folly not to recognize the fact. The Mexicans are *aboriginal Indians,* and they must share the destiny of their race."

This pre-Darwinian version of the "survival of the fittest" was branded by the aged Albert Gallatin, an opponent of the war, as "a most extraordinary assertion." That it persisted, that it constituted, in the 1850's, an integral part of the concept of manifest destiny is clear from the remarks of both friends and foes. John L. O'Sullivan was serving in 1855 as United States minister to Portugal. He reported to Secretary Marcy a conversation with some French imperialists in which he said:

"I should be as glad to see our common race and blood overspread all Africa under the French flag and all India under the British, as they ought to be to see it overspread all the Western hemisphere under ours;—and that probably enough that was the plan of Providence; to which we in America were accustomed to give the name of 'manifest destiny'."

On the other hand, George Fitzhugh of Virginia, who believed in institutions (such as slavery) for the protection of weaker races, charged the members of the "Young American" party in Congress with boasting "that the Anglo-Saxon race is manifestly destined to eat out all the other races, as the wire-grass destroys and takes the place of other grasses," and with inviting admiration for "this war of nature"—admiration which Fitzhugh, for one, refused to concede.

Thus manifest destiny, which must be thought of as embracing all the ideas hitherto considered—geographical determinism, the superiority of democratic institutions, the superior fecundity, stamina, and ability of the white race—became a justification for almost any addition of territory which the United States had the will and the power to obtain.

Such ideas were not, as has been rather generally assumed, peculiarly southern. In their extreme form, at least, both the ideas and the imperialistic program which they were used to justify were repudiated by southern Whig leaders, and even by John C. Calhoun himself. The southerner most closely associated with the program, Robert J. Walker, was of northern birth, was by no means an unwavering supporter of slavery, and was presently to sever entirely his connections with the South. The inventor of the phrase "manifest destiny" and one of the most perservering advocates of expansion was, as has been said, John L. O'Sullivan, who described himself in a letter to Calhoun as a "New York Free Soiler"; and he had the friendship and sympathy of prominent northern Democrats like Buchanan, Marcy, and Pierce. Indeed, if the manifest destiny of the 1840's and 1850's must be classified, it should be described as Democratic rather than sectional. Yet, even this generalization will not bear too close scrutiny, for William H. Seward, an antislavery Whig and Republican, was scarcely less intrigued by the idea than O'Sullivan himself. As early as 1846 he was predicting that the population of the United States was "destined to roll its resistless waves to the icy barriers of the North, and to encounter oriental civilization on the shores of the Pacific"; and in a speech at St. Paul, Minnesota, in 1860, he asserted with assurance that Russian, Canadian, and Latin on the American continents were but laying the foundations for the future states of the American republic, whose ultimate capital would be the City of Mexico.

Seward, in fact, supplies the chief link between the manifest destiny of the pre-Civil War years and the expansionist schemes of the decade following the war. As Secretary of State he had an opportunity to try his hand at a program of expansion; and though of all his plans the purchase of Alaska alone was carried through, the discussions of that and of other proposed acquisitions—the Danish West Indies, the Dominican Republic, the Hawaiian Islands, and Canada—demonstrated the continuity of ideas from 1850 to 1870. Professor T. C. Smith, who made an analysis of the expansionist arguments used in this period, found annexations urged on four principal grounds: economic value, strategic value to the navy, extension of republican institutions, and geographic determinism. Only the second of these—the naval base argument—was at all new. It owed its vogue at the time to the navy's difficulties during the war. The first was always to be met with, and the third and fourth were carry-overs from the days of manifest destiny.

The collapse of the expansionist program of Seward and Grant was followed by a general loss of interest in such enterprises, which did not recover their one-time popularity until the era of the Spanish-American War. In the meantime, however, new arguments were taking shape which would eventually impinge on the popular consciousness and raise almost as keen an interest in expansion as that which had elected Polk in 1844. But while manifest destiny was a product indigenous to the United States, some of the new doctrines owed their origin to European trends of thought.

In 1859 Charles Darwin published his *Origin of Species,* setting forth the hypothesis that the evolution of the higher forms of life had come about through the preservation and perpetuation of chance variations by the "survival of the fittest" in the never ending struggle for existence. . . .

What did Darwinism signify for the future of the United States? One of the first to attempt an answer to that riddle was the historian, John Fiske, who spoke with double authority as a student of American institutions and a follower and popularizer of Darwin. Fiske's conclusion was sufficiently gratifying. Anglo-Saxons in the United States had evolved the "fittest" of all political principles—federalism—upon which all the world would at some future day be organized. Anglo-Saxons, moreover, excelled not only in institutions but in growth of numbers and economic power. So evident was the superior "fitness" of this race that its expansion was certain to go on "until every land on the earth's surface that is not already the seat of an old civilization shall become English in its language, in its religion, in its political habits and traditions, and to a predominant extent in the blood of its people." "The day is at hand," said Fiske, "when four-fifths of the human race will trace its pedigree to English forefathers, as four-fifths of the white people of the United States trace their pedigree today." This was surely encouraging doctrine to Americans or British who wanted an excuse to go a-conquering.

Conclusions very similar to Fiske's were reached by Josiah Strong, a Congregational clergyman, who in 1885 published what became a popular and widely read book entitled *Our Country: Its Possible Future and Its Present Crisis.* The Anglo-Saxon, thought Strong, as the chief representative of the two most valuable civilizing forces—civil liberty and "a pure *spiritual* Christianity"—was being divinely schooled for *"the final competition of races. . . . ."* "If I read not amiss," he said, "this powerful race will move down upon Mexico, down upon Central and South America, out upon the islands of the sea, over upon Africa and beyond. And can any one doubt that the result of this competition of races will be the 'survival of the fittest'?" The extinction of inferior races before the conquering Anglo-Saxon might appear sad to some; but Strong knew of nothing likely to prevent it, and he accepted it as part of the divine plan. His doctrine was a curious blending of religious and scientific dogma.

If Fiske and Strong could show that expansion was a matter of destiny, another scholar of the day preached it as a duty. In his *Political Science and Comparative Constitutional Law,* published in 1890, John W. Burgess, of Columbia University, surveyed the political careers of the principal civilized races and concluded that, of them all, only the Teutonic group had talent of the highest order. Greek and Roman, Slav and Celt, had exhibited their various abilities. Some had excelled in building city-states; others, in planning world-empires. Only Teutons had learned the secret of the national state, the form fittest to survive. The Teutonic nations—German, and Anglo-Saxon—were "the political nations *par excellence*," and this pre-eminence gave them the right "in the economy of the world to assume the leadership in the establishment and administration of states."

Especially were they called "to carry the political civilization of the modern world into those parts of the world inhabited by unpolitical and barbaric races; i.e. they must have a colonial policy." There was "no human right to the status of barbarism." If barbaric peoples resisted the civilizing efforts of the political nations, the latter might rightly reduce them to subjection or clear their territory of their presence. If a population were not barbaric but merely incompetent politically, then too the Teutonic nations might "righteously assume sovereignty over, and undertake to create state order for, such a politically incompetent population."

There is in these pages of Burgess such a complete justification not only for British and German imperialism but also for the course of acquiring colonies and protectorates upon which the United States was to embark in 1898 that one learns with surprise from his rather naïve autobiography that Burgess was profoundly shocked by the war with Spain and felt that the adoption of an imperialistic career was a colossal blunder. One would have supposed that he would have rejoiced that his country was assuming its share of world responsibility as one of the Teutonic nations.

To Fiske and Strong, expansion was destiny; to Burgess, it was duty, though he apparently excused his own country from any share in its performance. To Alfred Thayer Mahan, the historian and prophet who frankly assumed the role of propagandist, it was both duty and opportunity. Mahan's *Influence of Sea Power upon History*, the result of a series of lectures at the Naval War College at Newport, Rhode Island, was published in 1890. Other books on naval history followed, but it is likely that Mahan reached a wider American public through the many magazine articles which he published at frequent intervals during the ensuing decade. History, as Mahan wrote it, was no mere academic exercise. Searching the past for lessons applicable to the here and now, he found them in full measure. Rather, he found *one*, which he never tired of driving home: Sea power was essential to national greatness. Sea power embraced commerce, merchant marine, navy, naval bases whence commerce might be protected, and colonies where it might find its farther terminals. One nation, Great Britain, had learned this lesson by heart and practiced it faithfully, with results that Mahan thought admirable. One other nation, he hoped, might walk in her footsteps.

Certain specific needs, beside the obvious one of a stronger navy and better coast defenses, Mahan urged upon his countrymen. If an Isthmian canal were to be built, the United States ought to build and control it, or, failing this, to control completely the approaches to it. This involved a willingness to accept islands in the Caribbean whenever they could be had by righteous means; sheer acts of conquest Mahan repudiated. It involved also a willingness to accept the Hawaiian Islands, partly as an outpost to the Pacific end of the canal, partly for another reason which weighed heavily with Mahan. The Pacific, he believed, was to be the theater of a vast conflict between Occident and Orient, with the United States holding the van of the Western forces. His deep religious sense assured him that the Deity was preparing the Christian powers for that coming cataclysm, but he was equally sure that mere human agents must keep their powder dry. The United States must be ready, with a navy, a canal, and as many island outposts as she could righteously acquire, for her share in the great struggle between civilizations and religions. Even the practical-minded naval officer must have a cosmic justification for the policy of national imperialism which he advocated.

It was such ideas as these of Fiske, Strong, Burgess, and Mahan which created a public opinion receptive to expansion overseas in 1898. . . .

Even those who stressed the economic value of new possessions could not refrain from claiming the special interest of Providence. That the war with Spain and the victory in the Philippines should have come just as the European powers were attempting to partition China and monopolize its markets, seemed to the *American Banker* of New York "a coincidence which has a providential air." Familiar to all students of the period is McKinley's story of how he prayed for divine guidance as to the disposition of the Philippines, and of how "one night it came to me this way—I don't know how it was but it came:

... that we could not turn them over to France or Germany—our commercial rivals in the Orient—that would be bad business and discreditable." Reasons of a more ideal character were vouchsafed to William McKinley on the same occasion, but McKinley's God did not hesitate to converse with him in terms that might better have befitted Mark Hanna. Perhaps McKinley did not misunderstand. Josiah Strong was a clergyman and hence in a better position than McKinley to interpret the wishes of the Deity; yet he found in Providence a concern for American business similar to that which McKinley detected. Strong, too, had in mind the Philippines and especially their relation to China and to the maintenance of the Open Door in the markets of that developing empire.

"And when we remember (he wrote) that our new necessities (markets for our manufacturers) are precisely complementary to China's new needs, it is not difficult to see a providential meaning in the fact that, with no design of our own, we have become an Asiatic power, close to the Yellow Sea, and we find it easy to believe that

'There's a divinity that shapes our ends,
Rough-hew them how we will.' "

Expansionists of different periods had invoked a God of Nature, a God of Democracy, a God of Evolution. It seems appropriate enough that those who inaugurated the last phase of territorial expansion, at the close of the nineteenth century, should have proclaimed their faith in a God of Business.

2 FROM　　　　　*Frederick Merk*

Imperialism Was the Antithesis of Manifest Destiny

Educated at Wisconsin and Harvard (Ph.D., 1920), Frederick Merk (1887–　　), also served as a member of the Inquiry, Woodrow Wilson's "brain trust," at the time of the Versailles Peace Conference. Succeeding his mentor, Frederick Jackson Turner, as the Harvard Historian of the American West, Merk is perhaps best known for his authoritative studies on the Oregon question in American diplomacy. Following his retirement, Merk's writings focused primarily on the concept of Manifest Destiny as an ideological continuum in American expansionist history. Compare his analysis of this theme with that of Pratt. How does he defend his thesis that the imperialism of the 1890's was the antithesis of the Manifest Destiny of the 1840's?

The imperialism of the 1890's is regarded by some historians as a variant merely of Manifest Destiny of the 1840's. This is an error. It was the antithesis of Manifest Destiny. Manifest Destiny was continentalism. It meant absorption of North America. It found its inspiration in states' rights. It envisaged the elevation of neighboring peoples to equal statehood and to all the rights and privileges which that guaranteed. Expansionism in 1899 was insular and imperialistic. Its inspiration was nationalism of a sort. It involved the reduction of distant peoples to a state of colonialism. It was what O'Sullivan had thundered against in his writings about Rome and England. It was what he had assured his readers America would never tolerate. Manifest Destiny had contained a principle so fundamental that a Calhoun and an O'Sullivan could agree on it—that a people not capable of rising to statehood should never be an-

SOURCE. Frederick Merk, *Manifest Destiny and Mission in American History*. Copyright 1963 by Frederick Merk, pp. 256–260. Reprinted by permission of Alfred A. Knopf, Inc.

nexed. That was the principle thrown overboard by the imperial-ists of 1899.

After the Spanish-American War, as after the Mexican War, expansionism lost attractiveness. The theory that growth is necessary to national life, as it is to individual life, that it is indispensable to vigor, and is a people's duty, even if it involves swallowing other people, fell into disfavor. A desire of an opposite course gradually replaced it, a wish to liquidate most, if not all, of the new empire as soon as was decently possible. Too much swallowing had, as usual, the effect of surfeit, weari-ness, and lethargy.

Cuba is a case in point. It had long been a goal of expansion-ists. In the 1840's and 1850's it had become a compelling attraction to them. In the 1890's some expansionists still hoped for it, though the interventionists in 1898 usually denied that they had a desire to acquire it. Senator Henry M. Teller, of Colorado, was of this group. He had been an exponent of Manifest Destiny for years. But he was unusual in his devotion to the principle of consent. He adhered to it more stubbornly than had his great predecessor, O'Sullivan. When the congres-sional resolution to intervene in Cuba reached the voting stage in the Senate he feared that some of his colleagues rushing to rescue the oppressed might yield to the temptation to keep the Pearl of the Antilles as reward for their labors. He proposed an amendment to the intervention resolution, pledging the United States to transfer sovereignty of the island to its people as soon as order had been restored. The amendment was easily passed in both houses without a recorded vote, a revealing evidence that as late as April 1898 Congress was not in an imperialist mood. Teller was hopeful that the Cuban people would have sense enough to ask admission to the Union after the war. They never had that sense.

In 1901, Congress, preparing for the withdrawal of the Army from the island, inserted stipulations in the Army appropriation bill. Cuba was to enter into no treaty, when once free, with another power which might impair her independence. She was to leave naval bases to the United States. The United States was to have a right to intervene in Cuba to maintain orderly government. These were the provisions of the Platt amendment, which Cubans perforce accepted. In later years these provisions were used to give validity to several interventions. But in 1934, in the days of Franklin D. Roosevelt, in line with his "Good Neighbor" policy, they were replaced by a treaty canceling all special rights of the United States in Cuba, with the exception of a lease of the naval base at Guantánamo Bay Thus, at last, in the liquidation of an empire, freedom came to the island which had been one of the earliest goals of Manifest Destiny.

The Philippine archipelago, which had been acquired as an afterthought of the war, was also kept in a status wherein its release was possible. It never was admitted into the bosom of the family with quite the warmth shown Hawaii. It was not made part of the United States by Congress in the sense in which the term "United States" is used in the Constitution. It was a possession of, an unincorporated part of, the United States. The restrictions placed on Congress in legislating for the United States proper did not apply to it. At least this is what the United States Supreme Court held in a major decision in 1904. In the decision use of the term "overseas colony" was avoided. The term used was "unincorporated territory," but it had a colonial look to it.

Democrats began demanding the liberation of the Philippines as early as the ratification of the treaty. They never did become reconciled to the view that national maturity inexorably required colonialism. In successive party platforms they urged that the islands go the way of Cuba. In the administration of Woodrow Wilson the Jones Act was passed, which gave dominion status to the islands as a first step toward independence. In 1933, over the veto of Herbert Hoover, Congress passed an independence act. But independence was not accepted by the legislature of the archipelago. However, satisfactory arrangements were eventually made, and on July 4, 1946, the Philippine Republic entered the community of free nations.

Others of the accessions of the period 1898–9 have had a different history. Hawaii, the most attractive of them, became linked to the mainland by ties of mutual interest and kindred population so close as almost to make her part of it. She had been "incorporated" into the United States by Congress as early as 1900. Her population kept up a persistent agitation for admission to statehood in the Union. In 1959 she was offered statehood, and by an overwhelming vote accepted it. Puerto

Rico, with a large Negro element in her population, became in 1952, with the consent of her people, a commonwealth associated with the United States. Guam, an advanced Pacific base, was administered by the Navy for a time. In 1950 the island obtained a civil government with a measure of local autonomy. Her function was that of defense, as was also that of other islands acquired at other times.

In this remodeling of empire, there emerged a pattern indicative of the true temper of the American people. A few islands—those necessary for defense—were retained. Those that were useful chiefly for commercial exploitation, such as the Philippines, were freed. Commercial exploitation had lost favor. It had proved injurious to some interests on the mainland, even if advantageous to others. For instance, the agitation for the independence of the Philippines was led by some of the sugar interests in the United States. The archipelago may be said to have been shown the door by sugar barons. In separating functions which colonies served—commercial from defense—and renouncing the first, Americans were repudiating their imperialists of 1899 who had merged the two for the greater glory of both. The stage was finally reached where Americans boasted, in a war of propaganda, of not being a colonial power at all, and looked askance at expansionists of their past who had conceived of the possessions of their neighbors as apples to be gathered in a basket.

3 FROM   *Richard Hofstadter*
America Was Engulfed by a Psychic Crisis

DeWitt Clinton Professor of American History at Columbia, Richard Hofstadter (1916–   ) is one of the most renowned historians of the modern era. Winner of the Beveridge Prize for Social Darwinism In American Thought, he has also won the Pulitzer Prize in two different categories for The Age of Reform and Anti-Intellectualism In American

SOURCE. Richard Hofstadter, *The Paranoid Style in American Politics and Other Essays.* Copyright 1952 by Richard Hofstadter, pp. 147-154, 159-161. Reprinted by permission of Alfred A. Knopf, Inc.

Life. The essay from which this selection was excerpted, was originally published in 1952, but it was substantially revised and enlarged in 1965 as a result of the challenges posed by the works of Ernest R. May, Walter LaFeber, and H. Wayne Morgan. Hofstadter, whose principal area of interest is the tradition of irrational activism endemic to American society, views the period 1893–1898 as an instructive case study in the dynamics of national emotion. But did the Panic of 1893 and the Venezuelan boundary dispute produce a public trauma of sufficient proportions to propel the country into war at an early date? If valid, does this analysis provide a useful insight into the complexities and confusions of contemporary American society?

The taking of the Philippine Islands from Spain in 1899 marked a major historical departure for the American people, a breach in their traditions and a shock to their established values. To be sure, from their national beginnings they had constantly engaged in expansion, but almost entirely into contiguous territory. Now they were extending themselves to distant extra-hemispheric colonies. They were abandoning a strategy of defense hitherto limited to the continent and its appurtenances, in favor of a major strategic commitment in the Far East. Thus far their expansion had been confined to the spread of a relatively homogeneous population into territories planned from the beginning to develop self-government; now control was to be imposed by force on millions of ethnic aliens. The acquisition of the islands, therefore, was understood by contemporaries on both sides of the debate, as it is readily understood today, to be a turning point in our history.

To discuss the debate in isolation from other events, however, would be to deprive it of its full significance. America's entrance into the Philippine Islands was a by-product of the Spanish-American War. The Philippine crisis is inseparable from the war crisis, and the war crisis itself is inseparable from a larger constellation that might be called "the psychic crisis of the 1890's."

Central in the background of the psychic crisis was the great depression that broke in 1893 and was still very acute when the agitation over the war in Cuba began. Severe depression, by itself, does not always generate an emotional crisis as intense as that of the nineties. In the 1870's the country had been swept by a depression of comparable acuteness and duration which, however, did not give rise to all the phenomena that appeared in the 1890's or to very many of them with comparable intensity and impact. It is often said that the 1890's, unlike the 1870's, form a "watershed" in American history. The difference between the emotional and intellectual impact of these two depressions can be measured, I believe, not by the difference in severity, but rather by reference to a number of singular events that in the 1890's converged with the depression to heighten its impact upon the public mind.

First in importance was the Populist movement, the freesilver agitation, the heated campaign of 1896. For the first time in our history a depression had created a protest movement strong enough to capture a major party and raise the specter, however unreal, of drastic social convulsion. Second was the maturation and bureaucratization of American business, the completion of its essential industrial plant, and the development of trusts on a scale sufficient to stir the anxiety that the old order of competitive opportunities was approaching an eclipse. Third, and of immense symbolic importance, was the apparent filling up of the continent and the disappearance of the frontier line. We now know how much land had not yet been taken up and how great were the remaining possibilities for internal expansion both in business and on the land; but to the mind of the 1890's it seemed that the resource that had engaged the energies of the people for three centuries had been used up. The frightening possibility suggested itself that a serious juncture in the nation's history had come. As Frederick Jackson Turner expressed it in his famous paper of 1893: "Now, four centuries from the discovery of America, at the end of one hundred years of life under the Constitution, the frontier has gone, and with its going has closed the first period of American history."

To middle-class citizens who had been brought up to think in terms of the nineteenth-century order, the outlook seemed grim. Farmers in the staple-growing region had gone mad over silver and Bryan; workers were stirring in bloody struggles like the Homestead and Pullman strikes; the supply of new land seemed at an end; the trust threatened the spirit of business enterprise; civic corruption was at a high point in the large cities; great waves of seemingly unassimilable immigrants arrived yearly and settled in hideous slums. To many historically conscious writers, the nation appeared overripe, like an empire ready for collapse through a stroke from outside or through internal upheaval. Acute as the situation was for all those who lived by the symbols of national power—for the governing and thinking classes—it was especially poignant for young people, who would have to make their careers in the dark world that seemed to be emerging.

The symptomatology of the crisis would record several tendencies in popular thought and behavior that had previously existed only in pale and tenuous form. These symptoms were manifest in two quite different moods. The key to one of them was an intensification of protest and humanitarian reform. Populism, utopianism, the rise of the Christian Social gospel, the growing intellectual interest in socialism, the social settlement movement that appealed so strongly to the college generation of the nineties, the quickening of protest and social criticism in the realistic novel—all these are expressions of this mood. The other mood was one of national self-assertion, aggression, expansion. The motif of the first was social sympathy; of the second, national power. During the 1890's far more patriotic groups were founded than in any other decade of our history; the naval theories of Captain Mahan were gaining in influence; naval construction was booming; there was an immense quickening of the American cult of Napoleon and a vogue of the virile and martial writings of Rudyard Kipling; young Theodore Roosevelt became the exemplar of the vigorous, masterful, out-of-doors man; the revival of European imperialism stirred speculation over what America's place would be in the world of renewed colonial rivalries, and in some stirred a demand to get into the imperial race to avoid the risk of being overwhelmed by other powers. But most significant was the rising tide of jingoism, a matter of constant comment among observers of American life during the decade.

Jingoism, of course, was not new in American history. But during the 1870's and the 1880's the American public had been notably quiescent about foreign relations. There had been expansionist statesmen, but they had been blocked by popular apathy, and our statecraft had been restrained. Grant had failed dismally in his attempt to acquire Santo Domingo; our policy toward troubled Hawaii had been cautious; in 1877 an offer of two Haitian naval narbors had been spurned. In responding to Haiti, Secretary of State Frelinghuysen had remarked that "the policy of this Government . . . has tended toward avoidance of possessions disconnected from the main continent." Henry Cabot Lodge, in his life of George Washington published in 1889, observed that foreign relations then filled "but a slight place in American politics, and excite generally only a languid interest." Within a few years this comment would have seemed absurd. In 1895, Russell A. Alger reported to Lodge, after reading one of Lodge's own articles to a Cincinnati audience, that he was convinced by the response that foreign policy, "more than anything else, touches the public pulse of today." The history of the 1890's is the history of public agitation over expansionist issues and of quarrels with other nations.

Three primary incidents fired American jingoism between the spring of 1891 and the close of 1895. First came Secretary of State Blaine's tart and provocative reply to the Italian minister's protest over the lynching of eleven Italians in New Orleans. Then there was friction with Chile over a riot in Valparaíso in which two American sailors were killed and several injured by a Chilean mob. In 1895 occurred the more famous Venezuela boundary dispute with Britain. Discussion of these incidents would take us too ·far afield, but note that they all had these characteristics in common: in none of them was national security or the national interest vitally and immediately involved; in all three American diplomacy was extraordinarily and disproportionately aggressive; in all three the possibility of war was contemplated; and in each case the response of the American public and press was enthusiastically nationalist and almost unanimous.

It is hard to read the history of these events without concluding that politicians were persistently using jingoism to restore their prestige, mend their party fences, and divert the public mind from grave internal discontents. It hardly seems an accident that jingoism and populism rose together. Documentary evidence for the political exploitation of foreign crises is not overwhelmingly abundant, in part because such a motive is not necessarily conscious and where it is conscious it is not always confessed or recorded. The persistence of jingoism in every administration from Harrison's to Theodore Roosevelt's, however, is too suggestive to be ignored. During the nineties the press of each party was fond of accusing the other of exploiting foreign conflict. Blaine was not above twisting the British lion's tail for political purposes; and it is hardly likely that he would have exempted Italy from the same treatment. Harrison, on the eve of the Chile affair, for the acuteness of which he was primarily responsible, was being urged by prominent Republican politicians who had the coming presidential campaign in mind to pursue a more aggressive foreign policy because it would "have the . . . effect of diverting attention from stagnant political discussions." And although some Democratic papers charged that he was planning to run for reelection during hostilities so that he could use the "don't swap horses in the middle of the stream" appeal, many Democrats felt that it was politically necessary for them to back him against Chile so that, as one of their congressmen remarked, the Republicans could not "run away with all the capital there is to be made in an attempt to assert national self-respect."

Grover Cleveland was a man of exceptional integrity whose stand against pressure for the annexation of Hawaii during 1893–4 does him much credit. But precisely for this act of restraint he was accused by Republican jingoes like Lodge and by many in his own party of being indifferent to America's position in the world. And if Cleveland was too high-minded a man to exploit a needless foreign crisis, his Secretary of State, Richard Olney, was not. The Venezuela affair, which came at a low point in the prestige of Cleveland's administration, offered Olney a rich chance to prove to critics in both parties that the administration was, after all, capable of vigorous diplomacy. That the crisis might have partisan value was not unthinkable to members of Olney's party. He received a letter from a Texas congressman encouraging him to "go ahead," on the ground that the Venezuela issue was a "winner" in every section of the country.

"When you come to diagnose the country's internal ills," his correspondent continued, "the possibilities of 'blood and iron' loom up immediately. Why, Mr. Secretary, just think of how angry the anarchistic, socialistic, and populistic boil appears on our political surface and who knows how deep its roots extend or ramify? One cannon shot across the bow of a British boat in defense of this principle will knock more *pus* out of it than would suffice to inoculate and corrupt our people for the next two centuries."

This pattern had been well established when the Cuban crisis broke out anew in 1895. . . .

I suspect that the readiness of the public to overreact to the Cuban situation can be understood in part through the displacement of feelings of sympathy or social protest generated in domestic affairs; these impulses found a safe and satisfactory discharge in foreign conflict. Spain was portrayed in the press as waging a heartless and inhuman war; the Cubans were portrayed as noble victims of Spanish tyranny, their situation as analogous to that of Americans in 1776. When one examines the sectional and political elements that were most enthusiastic about policies that led to war, one finds them not primarily among the wealthy eastern big-business Republicans who gave McKinley his strongest support and read the dignified conservative newspapers, but in the Bryan sections of the country, in the Democratic party, among western Republicans, and among the readers of the yellow journals. A great many businessmen were known to fear the effects of a war on the prosperity that was just returning, and some thought that a war might strengthen the free-silver movement. During the controversy significant charges were hurled back and forth: conservative peace advocates claimed that many jingoists were hoping for a costly war over Cuba that could be made the occasion of a return to free silver; in reply, the inflammatory press often fell into the pattern of Populist rhetoric, declaiming, for example, about "the eminently respectable porcine citizens who—for dollars in the money-grubbing sty, support 'conservative' newspapers and consider the starvation of . . . inoffensive men, women and children, and the murder of 250 American sailors . . . of less importance than a fall of two points in a price of stocks." As Margaret Leech has remarked, peace "had become a symbol of obedience to avarice." In the case of some of the war enthusiasts it is not clear whether they favored action more because they bled for the sufferings of the Cubans or because they hated the materialism and the flaccid pacifism of the *haute bourgeoisie*. Theodore Roosevelt, who was not in the habit of brooding over the wrongs done to the underdog in the United States, expressed some of this when he cried at Mark Hanna: "We will have this war for the freedom of Cuba in spite of the timidity of the commercial interests."

Although imputations of base motives were made by both sides, it is also significant that the current of sympathy and agitation ran strong where a discontented constituency, chagrined at Bryan's defeat, was most numerous. An opportunity to discharge hatred of "Wall Street interests" that were coolly indifferent to the fate of both Cuban *insurrectos* and staple farmers may have been more important than the more rationalized and abstract linkage between war and free silver. The primary significance of this war in the psychic economy of the 1890's was that it served as an outlet for expressing aggressive impulses while presenting itself, quite truthfully, as an idealistic and humanitarian crusade. It had the advantage of expressing in one issue both the hostilities and the generous moral passions of the public. The American public on the whole showed little interest in such material gains as might accrue from an intervention in Cuba. It never dreamed that the war would lead to the taking of the Philippines, of whose existence it was hardly aware. Starting a war for a high-minded and altruistic purpose and then transmuting it into a war for annexation was unimaginable. That would be, as McKinley put it in a phrase that later came back to haunt him, "criminal aggression."

4 FROM   *William A. Williams*

Economic Motives Were the Decisive Factors

*A graduate of the U.S. Naval Academy and Wisconsin (Ph.D., 1950),
William A. Williams (1921–   ) taught at the latter school for many
years before moving to Oregon State. Dismissed by many of his critics
as a neo-Beardian or a Marxist determinist because of his emphasis
on economic factors in the interpretation of the American past, he
is regarded by others as one of the most influential diplomatic historians
of recent decades, because of his adaptation of the Clausewitzian notion
that foreign policy is a conscious extension of domestic policy decisions.
In this selection note the emphasis Williams places on the calculated
working relationship between business and government in the promotion of American expansionist policies. If this forces one to reconsider the Hofstadter analysis, the question must still be asked: Is
economic motivation an all-embracing explanation of the events of
1893–1898?*

Clearly the most significant of the factors was the consensus
among business leaders on the absolute necessity of overseas expansion. Even before he had become a presidential candidate,
for example, the National Association of Manufacturers chose
McKinley to keynote their organizational meeting in 1895 of
"the large manufacturers who are engaged in foreign trade."
Acting on the axiom that such overseas economic expansion
offered the "only promise of relief" to the now perpetual existence of vast surpluses, the N.A.M. stressed the need of vigorous
government support and the usefulness of reciprocity treaties in
obtaining cheap raw materials as well as new export markets.
McKinley had modified his support of high tariffs in line with
the more sophisticated views of former Secretary of State James G.

SOURCE. William A. Williams, *The Contours of American History*, pp.
363–367. Copyright 1961 by William Appleman Williams. Reprinted by permission of The World Publishing Company and Jonathan Cape Limited.

Blaine as a way of satisfying Ohio businessmen who demanded access to overseas markets. "It is a mighty problem to keep the whole of industry in motion," he explained in 1895, and concluded that it "cannot be kept in motion without markets." Moving vigorously once it was organized, the N.A.M. established its own warehouses and agents in Asia and Latin America and began an ultimately successful campaign for government assistance in entering and developing such markets.

McKinley gave the featured address at the 1897 meeting of the Philadelphia Commercial Museum, also organized to push overseas economic expansion. "No worthier cause (than) the expansion of trade," he asserted, " . . . can engage our energies at this hour." Flour millers, wool manufacturers, the National Live Stock Exchange, and the Committee on American Interests in China (which soon became the American Asiatic Association) added their enthusiastic agreement—and their vigorous pressure on the government. Journals like *Scientific American, Engineering Magazine,* and *Iron Age* asked for relief in the same form. But McKinley himself provided the most succinct summary of the whole movement. "We want our own markets for our manufactures and agricultural products"; he explained in 1895, "we want a foreign market for our surplus products. . . . We want a reciprocity which will give us foreign markets for our surplus products, and in turn that will open our markets to foreigners for those products which they produce and which we do not."

Other politicians and intellectuals extended the expand-or-stagnate approach to the American economy to include all aspects of American life. Church leaders resolved the conflict between pseudo-science and religion by merging and transforming them in a supercharged reforming imperialism. Congregationalist Josiah Strong thought it "manifest" that the American branch of the Anglo-Saxon family would move out into the new frontiers of the world with righteous benevolence. "It would seem," he concluded, "as if these inferior tribes were only precursors of a superior race, voices in the wilderness crying: Prepare ye the way of the Lord." In his view (shared or adapted by others like John Fiske), America was the chosen instrument of a white, Protestant, Anglo-Saxon Jehovah whose master plan was an earlier version of Darwinism.

Several historians presented secular versions of the same basic argument. Though originally an anti-imperialist, naval officer Alfred Thayer Mahan was converted to empire by a combination of the Navy's own interest and his reading of (and borrowing from) English and French mercantilists. Though his influence has often been exaggerated, Mahan's neat formula for producing domestic wealth, welfare, and morality through exports protected by a big navy did enjoy wide popularity and provided a convenient way of talking about empire in terms of ethics and defense.

Though he was almost unknown to the general public, Brooks Adams was more original than Mahan and also exerted considerable influence on foreign policy leaders like Richard Olney, John Hay, Henry Cabot Lodge, and Theodore Roosevelt. Arguing from his study of history that great civilizations were created by conquering, organizing, and integrating huge slices of the world's western frontier, Adams concluded that the center of empire had in the 1890s reached the United States. In order to maintain that position, the nation had therefore to abandon laissez faire, accept the corporation political economy, organize it rationally and effectively, and expand it by tightening up control of the Western Hemisphere and winning economic dominance of Asia. Desperately concerned to avoid a revolution that would bring socialism, or perhaps simply anarchy, Adams openly avowed his imperialism. "I take it our destiny is to reorganize the Asiatic end of the vast chaotic mass we call Russia." He enthused at the prospect. "And, by God, I like it."

Far less openly imperialist, though by no means opposed to expansion, Frederick Jackson Turner developed a narrower and more specifically American version of the frontier thesis. Expansion had made Americans democratic and prosperous. The implication was clear: no more frontiers, no more wealth and welfare. Though Turner remained primarily a historian and seldom entered the arena of public debate or the dens of private influence, many public figures immediately recognized that he was saying the same thing as the corporation leaders, even though he was phrasing it in the rhetoric of the middle class. Men as different as Theodore Roosevelt, who had also written about the conquest of the West, the editors of the *Atlantic Monthly,* and a young intellectual named Woodrow Wilson who aspired to political power saw this meaning and significance in Turner's interpretation and adopted it as their own. And in subsequent decades, the idea that new and expanding frontiers provided the solution to America's difficulties became one of the nation's basic and persuasive assumptions. It influenced the outlook of men as different as Nelson Rockefeller and Henry Wallace as well as their respective peers, together with less famous but none the less important policy-makers.

Each of these major ideas, from the conception of the new system as depending upon an expanding market place to Turner's frontier thesis, reinforced and extended the others, and taken together they made sense out of the multiplicity of particularistic demands for expansion. *Given this expansionist theory of prosperity and history, the activities of foreign nations were interpreted almost wholly as events which denied the United States the opportunity for its vital expansion. A different explanation of the nation's difficulties would have produced a different estimate of foreign actions, for not one of the countries actually threatened the United States* [author's italics].

But when European nations like France, Germany, and Austria raised tariff barriers against American surpluses, the act was viewed as threatening American wealth and welfare. Not even England escaped a share of the blame. For though it was clearly deciding that it would be wise to work out an underlying entente with America, England gave no evidence that it would cease to compete with the United States within that framework. And in Asia, where China was rapidly coming to be defined as the vital new frontier of American prosperity and democracy, Japan and Russia were seen as joining England and France (and even Germany and Italy) in dividing the opportunities among themselves and thereby excluding the United States. McKinley agreed with Cleveland's conclusion that the Asian crisis "deserves our gravest consideration by reason of its disturbance of our growing commercial interests." And both were intimately familiar with the requests from corporation leaders for "energetic" action "for the preservation and portection of (our) important commercial interests in that (Chinese) Empire."

Up to the spring and summer of 1897, therefore, American

foreign policy was largely taken up with an expansionist drive directed toward Asia. Spain's difficulties in Cuba were a matter of official concern and sporadic popular interest, but not even Joseph Pulitzer and William Randolph Hearst managed to whip up any sustained excitement or pressure for intervention. As they later admitted, both newspaper publishers were acting as narrow interest-conscious operators concerned with their circulation figures (and hence advertising revenues). They were classic examples of the irresponsibility of the new mass-merchandising approach to information. While they undoubtedly created an emotional concern in the winter and spring of 1897–1898 to save Cuba, neither they nor their readers made the decision to go to war.

That was done by McKinley and a few close advisors on the grounds that specific and general American interests could not be satisfied by any other course. Hence to explain the Spanish-American War as inevitable is to engage in an intellectual and moral evasion of the entire problem. America was vastly more powerful than Spain. And the definition of America's needs made by its own leaders produced the war. To conclude that such a definition was also inevitable is to resort to nonhistorical reasoning. For being able to explain how that outlook arose in the minds of American leaders is not at all to prove that no other view could have developed.

Against the background, and in the context, of the consensus on expansion, several factors combined to shift primary attention from China to Cuba. American corporations with direct economic interests in the island launched a vigorous campaign for intervention. At the same time, many people who had favored the revolution began to change their minds. Becoming skeptical of its nature and purposes, they preferred intervention to support moderate and conservative elements. By the late fall of 1897, moreover, many large corporation leaders who had opposed war up to that time began to feel that the situation had to be stabilized so that domestic recovery and overseas expansion could proceed without further delay and interruption.

Sharing this estimate, the McKinley Administration had already advised the Spanish as early as November 20, 1897, that "peace in Cuba is necessary to the welfare of the people of the United States." Having defined the problem in those terms, McKinley on December 6, 1897, graciously gave Spain "a reasonable chance" to do what he told them. But in complying with American pressure to replace a military commander who was in fact restoring order, Madrid only made it impossible for itself to comply with the basic demand. For less determined military operations allowed the rebels to recoup some of their losses. Stalemate was the result. America had thus irresponsibly demanded results while denying Spain the right to use effective means. Impatient of further delay, and cavalierly deprecating Spain's continued efforts to meet his demands, McKinley went to war to remove the distraction, establish firm control of the Caribbean, and proceed with expansion into Asia.

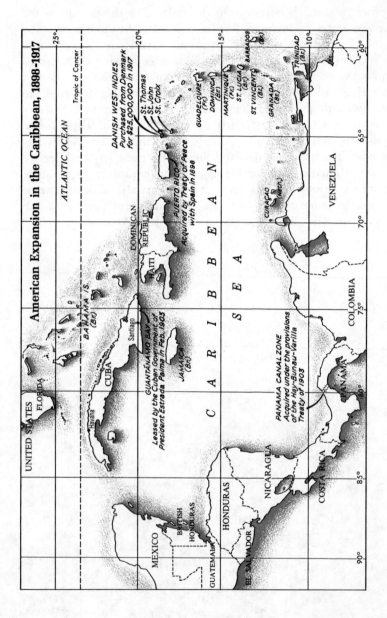

American Expansion in the Caribbean, 1898-1917

UNITED STATES
FLORIDA
ATLANTIC OCEAN
Tropic of Cancer

BAHAMA IS.
(Br.)

Havana
CUBA
Santiago

GUANTÁNAMO BAY
Leased by the Cuban Government or
President Estrada Palma in Feb., 1903

JAMAICA
(Br.)

C A R I B B E A N   S E A

MEXICO

BRITISH
HONDURAS

GUATEMALA

HONDURAS

EL SALVADOR
NICARAGUA

COSTA RICA

PANAMA

PANAMA CANAL ZONE
Acquired under the provisions
of the Hay-Bunau-Varilla
Treaty of 1903

HAITI
DOMINICAN
REPUBLIC

PUERTO RICO
Acquired by Treaty of Peace
with Spain in 1898

DANISH WEST INDIES
Purchased from Denmark
for $25,000,000 in 1917
St. Thomas
St. John
St. Croix

GUADELOUPE
(Fr.)
DOMINICA
(Br.)

MARTINIQUE
(Fr.)
ST. LUCIA
(Br.)
ST. VINCENT
(Br.)
GRANADA
(Br.)
BARBADOS
(Br.)

CURAÇAO
(Neth.)

TRINIDAD
(Br.)

COLOMBIA

VENEZUELA

90°   85°   80°   75°   70°   65°   60°
25°   20°   15°   10°

PART TWO

The Decision for War Against Spain

THE DECISION FOR WAR AGAINST SPAIN

5   *Grover Cleveland*

*Cleveland's View of the Cuban Crisis,
7 December 1896*

Stephen Grover Cleveland (1837–1908), the only Democratic President to serve (1885–1889 and 1893–1897) between Buchanan and Wilson, has fared exceptionally well at the hands of historians, most of whom have been unduly influenced by the sympathetic Pulitzer Prize biography by Allan Nevins. However, Cleveland's foreign policy with respect to Hawaii, Venezuela, and Cuba has been negatively reassessed in the years since 1961 by a new generation of historians who refuse to accept a 'sudden aberration' or "jingo" thesis as a ready rationale for the events of 1898. In this Presidential analysis of U.S. policy regarding the Cuban insurrection, note Cleveland's emphasis on the American economic stake in that troubled isle, and the implied threat of formal American intervention. Is this consonant with the traditional interpretation of Cleveland as an anti-Big Business, pacifist President?

The insurrection in Cuba still continues with all its perplexities. It is difficult to perceive that any progress has thus far been made towards the pacification of the island or that the situation

SOURCE. Stephen Grover Cleveland, "Annual Message of the President of the United States," dated 7 December 1896, in *Papers Relating to the Foreign Relations of the United States, 1896,* Washington: Government Printing Office, 1897, pp. xxix–xxxvi *passim.*

of affairs as depicted in my last annual message has in the least improved. If Spain still holds Havana and the seaports and all the considerable towns, the insurgents still roam at will over at least two-thirds of the inland country. If the determination of Spain to put down the insurrection seems but to strengthen with the lapse of time, and is evinced by her unhesitating devotion of largely increased military and naval forces to the task, there is much reason to believe that the insurgents have gained in point of numbers, and character, and resources, and are none the less inflexible in their resolve not to succumb, without practically securing the great objects for which they took up arms. If Spain has not yet reestablished her authority, neither have the insurgents yet made good their title to be regarded as an independent state. Indeed, as the contest has gone on, the pretense that civil government exists on the island, except so far as Spain is able to maintain it, has been practically abandoned. Spain does keep on foot such a government, more or less imperfectly, in the large towns and their immediate suburbs. But, that exception being made, the entire country is either given over to anarchy or is subject to the military occupation of one or the other party. It is reported, indeed, on reliable authority that, at the demand of the commander in chief of the insurgent army, the putative Cuban government has now given up all attempt to exercise its functions, leaving that government confessedly (what there is the best reason for supposing it always to have been in fact) a government merely on paper.

Were the Spanish armies able to meet their antagonists in the open, or in pitched battle, prompt and decisive results might be looked for, and the immense superiority of the Spanish forces in numbers, discipline, and equipment, could hardly fail to tell greatly to their advantage. But they are called upon to face a foe that shuns general engagements, that can choose and does choose its own ground, that from the nature of the country is visible or invisible at pleasure, and that fights only from ambuscade and when all the advantages of position and numbers are on its side. In a country where all that is indispensable to life in the way of food, clothing, and shelter is so easily obtainable, especially by those born and bred on the soil, it is obvious that there is hardly a limit to the time during which hostilities of this sort may be prolonged. Meanwhile, as in all cases of protracted civil strife, the passions of the combatants grow more and more inflamed and excesses on both sides become more frequent and more deplorable. They are also participated in by bands of marauders, who, now in the name of one party and now in the name of the other, as may best suit the occasion, harry the country at will and plunder its wretched inhabitants for their own advantage. Such a condition of things would inevitably entail immense destruction of property even if it were the policy of both parties to prevent it as far as practicable. But while such seemed to be the original policy of the Spanish Government, it has now apparently abandoned it and is acting upon the same theory as the insurgents, namely, that the exigencies of the contest require the wholesale annihilation of property, that it may not prove of use and advantage to the enemy. . . .

The spectacle of the utter ruin of an adjoining country, by nature one of the most fertile and charming on the globe, would engage the serious attention of the Government and people of the United States in any circumstances. In point of fact, they have a concern with it which is by no means of a wholly sentimental or philanthropic character. It lies so near to us as to be hardly separated from our territory. Our actual pecuniary interest in it is second only to that of the people and Government of Spain. It is reasonably estimated that at least from $30,000,000 to $50,000,000 of American capital are invested in plantations and in railroad, mining, and other business enterprises on the island. The volume of trade between the United States and Cuba, which in 1889 amounted to about $64,000,000, rose in 1893 to about $103,000,000, and in 1894, the year before the present insurrection broke out, amounted to nearly $96,-000,000. Besides this large pecuniary stake in the fortunes of Cuba, the United States finds itself inextricably involved in the present contest in other ways both vexatious and costly. . . .

These inevitable entanglements of the United States with the rebellion in Cuba, the large American property interests affected, and considerations of philanthropy and humanity in general, have led to a vehement demand in various quarters, for some sort of positive intervention on the part of the United States. It was at first proposed that belligerent rights should be accorded to the insurgents—a proposition no longer urged because untimely and in practical operation clearly perilous and injurious to our own interests. It has since been and is now sometimes contended that the independence of the insurgents should be recognized. But imperfect and restricted as the Spanish government of the island may be, no other exists there—unless the will of the military officer in temporary command of a particular district, can be dignified as a species of government. It is now also suggested that the United States should buy the island—a suggestion possibly worthy of consideration if there were any evidence of a desire or willingness on the part of Spain to entertain such a proposal. It is urged, finally, that, all other methods failing, the existing internecine strife in Cuba should be terminated by our intervention, even at the cost of a war between the United States and Spain—a war which its advocates confidently prophesy could be neither large in its proportions nor doubtful in its issue.

The correctness of this forecast need be neither affirmed nor denied. The United States has nevertheless a character to maintain as a nation, which plainly dictates that right and not might should be the rule of its conduct. Further, though the United States is not a nation to which peace is a necessity, it is in truth the most pacific of powers, and desires nothing so much as to live in amity with all the world. Its own ample and diversified domains satisfy all possible longings for territory, preclude all dreams of conquest, and prevent any casting of covetous eyes upon neighboring regions, however attractive. That our conduct towards Spain and her dominions has constituted no exception to this national disposition is made manifest by the course of our Government, not only thus far during the present insurrection, but during the ten years that followed the rising at Yara in 1868. No other great power, it may safely be said, under circumstances of similar perplexity, would have manifested the same restraint and the same patient endurance. It may also be said that this persistent attitude of the United States towards Spain in connection with Cuba, unquestionably evinces no slight respect and regard for Spain on the part of the American people. They in truth do not forget her connection with the discovery of the Western Hemisphere, nor do they underestimate the great qualities of the Spanish people, nor fail to fully recognize their splendid patriotism and their chivalrous devotion to the national honor. . . .

It would seem that if Spain should offer to Cuba genuine autonomy—a measure of home rule which, while preserving the sovereignty of Spain, would satisfy all rational requirements of her Spanish subjects—there should be no just reason why the pacification of the island might not be effected on that basis. Such a result would appear to be in the true interest of all concerned. It would at once stop the conflict which is now consuming the resources of the island and making it worthless for whichever party may ultimately prevail. It would keep intact the possessions of Spain without touching her honor, which will be consulted rather than impugned by the adequate redress of admitted grievances. It would put the prosperity of the island and the fortunes of its inhabitants within their own control, without severing the natural and ancient ties which bind them to the mother country, and would yet enable them to test their capacity for self-government under the most favorable conditions. It has been objected on the one side that Spain should not promise autonomy until her insurgent subjects lay down their arms; on the other side, that promised autonomy, however liberal, is insufficient, because without assurance of the promise being fulfilled. . . .

Nevertheless, realizing that suspicions and precautions on the part of the weaker of two combatants are always natural and not always unjustifiable—being sincerely desirous in the interest of both as well as on its own account that the Cuban problem should be solved with the least possible delay—it was intimated by this Government to the Government of Spain some months ago that, if a satisfactory measure of home rule were tendered the Cuban insurgents, and would be accepted by them upon a guaranty of its execution, the United States would endeavor to find a way not objectionable to Spain of furnishing such guaranty. While no definite response to this intimation has yet been received from the Spanish Government, it is believed to be not altogether unwelcome, while, as already suggested, no reason is perceived why it should not be approved by the insurgents. Neither party can fail to see the importance of early action and both must realize that to prolong the present state of things for even a short period will add enormously to the time and labor and expenditure necessary to bring about the industrial recuperation of the island. It is therefore fervently hoped on all grounds that earnest efforts for healing the breach between Spain and the insurgent Cubans, upon the lines above indicated, may be at once inaugurated and pushed to an immediate and successful issue. The friendly offices of the United States, either in the manner above outlined or in any other way consistent with our Constitution and laws, will always be at the disposal of either party.

Whatever circumstances may arise, our policy and our interests would constrain us to object to the acquisition of the island or an interference with its control by any other power.

It should be added that it can not be reasonably assumed that the hitherto expectant attitude of the United States will be indefinitely maintained. While we are anxious to accord all due respect to the sovereignty of Spain, we can not view the pending conflict in all its features, and properly apprehend our inevitably close relations to it, and its possible results, without considering that by the course of events we may be drawn into such an unusual and unprecedented condition, as will fix a limit to our patient waiting for Spain to end the contest, either alone and in her own way, or with our friendly cooperation.

When the inability of Spain to deal successfully with the insurrection has become manifest, and it is demonstrated that her sovereignty is extinct in Cuba for all purposes of its rightful existence, and when a hopeless struggle for its reestablishment has degenerated into strife which means nothing more than the useless sacrifice of human life and the utter destruction of the very subject-matter of the conflict, a situation will be presented in which our obligations to the sovereignty of Spain will be superseded by higher obligations, which we can hardly hesitate to recognize and discharge. Deferring the choice of ways and methods until the time for action arrives, we should make them depend upon the precise conditions then existing; and they should not be determined upon without giving careful heed to every consideration involving our honor and interest, or the international duty we owe to Spain. Until we face the contingencies suggested, or the situation is by other incidents imperatively changed, we should continue in the line of conduct heretofore pursued, thus in all circumstances exhibiting our obedience to the requirements of public law and our regard for the duty enjoined upon us by the position we occupy in the family of nations.

A contemplation of emergencies that may arise should plainly lead us to avoid their creation, either through a careless disregard of present duty or even an undue stimulation and ill-timed expression of feeling. But I have deemed it not amiss to remind the Congress that a time may arrive when a correct policy and care for our interests, as well as a regard for the interests of other nations and their citizens, joined by considerations of humanity and a desire to see a rich and fertile country, intimately related to us, saved from complete devastation, will constrain our Government to such action as will subserve the interests thus involved and at the same time promise to Cuba and its inhabitants an opportunity to enjoy the blessings of peace.

6   *William McKinley*

McKinley's View of the Cuban Crisis, 6 December 1897

Interestingly, William McKinley (1843–1901), often regarded as the stereotype of fainéant Republican presidents in the post-Civil War period, has been historiographically rehabilitated in the years since 1959, as a result of the researches of Margaret Leech, H. Wayne Morgan,

SOURCE. William McKinley, "Annual Message of the President of the United States," dated 6 December 1897, in *Papers Relating to the Foreign Relations of the United States, 1897,* Washington: Government Printing Office, 1898, pp. xi–xx.

and Walter LaFeber, among others. McKinley, in the main, continued the Cleveland policies of putting pressure on the Madrid government while refusing to grant formal belligerent status to the Cuban insurgents. The assassination of the conservative Spanish Prime Minister, Antonio Cánovas del Castillo, on 8 August 1897, and the accession to power of a liberal coalition government headed by Praxedes Mateo Sagasta as Prime Minister and Segismundo Moret as Minister for Colonies, provided a temporary respite and increased hope for effecting a diplomatic détente. In spite of this, note the pessimism implicit in McKinley's message, and his public awareness of the foreclosure of certain American diplomatic options. Compare his analysis of the Cuban crisis with that of Cleveland. Which seems more bellicose?

The most important problem with which this Government is now called upon to deal pertaining to its foreign relations concerns its duty toward Spain and the Cuban insurrection. Problems and conditions more or less in common with those now existing have confronted this Government at various times in the past. The story of Cuba for many years has been one of unrest; growing discontent; an effort toward a larger enjoyment of liberty and self-control; of organized resistance to the mother country; of depression after distress and warfare and of ineffectual settlement to be followed by renewed revolt. For no enduring period since the enfranchisement of the continental possessions of Spain in the Western continent has the condition of Cuba or the policy of Spain toward Cuba not caused concern to the United States. . . .

The existing conditions can not but fill this Government and the American people with the gravest apprehension. There is no desire on the part of our people to profit by the misfortunes of Spain. We have only the desire to see the Cubans prosperous and contented, enjoying that measure of self-control which is the inalienable right of man, protected in their right to reap the benefit of the exhaustless treasures of their country.

The offer made by my predecessor in April, 1896, tendering the friendly offices of this Government failed. Any mediation on our part was not accepted. In brief the answer read: "There is no effectual way to pacify Cuba unless it begins with the actual submission of the rebels to the mother country." Then only could Spain act in the promised direction, of her own motion and after her own plans.

The cruel policy of concentration was initiated February 16, 1896. The productive districts controlled by the Spanish armies were depopulated. The agricultural inhabitants were herded in and about the garrison towns, their lands laid waste and their dwellings destroyed. This policy the late Cabinet of Spain justified as a necessary measure of war and as a means of cutting off supplies from the insurgents. It has utterly failed as a war measure. It was not civilized warfare. It was extermination.

Against this abuse of the rights of war I have felt constrained on repeated occasions to enter the firm and earnest protest of this Government. There was much of public condemnation of the treatment of American citizens by alleged illegal arrests and long imprisonment awaiting trial or pending protracted judicial proceedings. I felt it my first duty to make instant demand for the release or speedy trial of all American citizens under arrest. Before the change of the Spanish Cabinet in October last twenty-two prisoners, citizens of the United States, had been given their freedom.

For the relief of our own citizens suffering because of the conflict the aid of Congress was sought in a special message, and under the appropriation of April 4, 1897, effective aid has been given to American citizens in Cuba, many of them at their own request having been returned to the United States.

The instructions given to our new Minister to Spain before this departure for his post directed him to impress upon that Government the sincere wish of the United States to lend its aid toward the ending of the war in Cuba by reaching a peaceful and lasting result, just and honorable alike to Spain and to the Cuban people. These instructions recited the character and duration of the contest, the widespread losses it entails, the burdens and restraints it imposes upon us, with constant disturbance of National interests, and the injury resulting from an indefinite continuance of this state of things. It was stated that at this juncture our Government was constrained to seriously inquire if the time was not ripe when Spain of her own volition, moved by her own interests and every sentiment of humanity, should put a stop to this destructive war and make proposals of settlement honorable to herself and just to her Cuban colony. It was urged that as a neighboring nation, with large interests in Cuba, we could be required to wait only a reasonable time for the mother country to establish its authority and restore peace and order within the borders of the Island; that we could not contemplate an indefinite period for the accomplishment of this result.

No solution was proposed to which the slightest idea of humiliation to Spain could attach, and indeed precise proposals were withheld to avoid embarrassment to that Government. All that was asked or expected was that some safe way might be speedily provided and permanent peace restored. It so chanced that the consideration of this offer, addressed to the same Spanish Administration which had declined the tenders of my predecessor and which for more than two years had poured men and treasure into Cuba in the fruitless effort to suppress the revolt, fell to others. Between the departure of General Woodford, the new Envoy, and his arrival in Spain the statesman who had shaped the policy of his country fell by the hand of an assassin, and although the Cabinet of the late Premier still held office and received from our Envoy the proposals he bore, that Cabinet gave place within a few days thereafter to a new Administration, under the leadership of Sagasta.

The reply to our note was received on the 23d day of October. It is in the direction of a better understanding. It appreciates the friendly purposes of this Government. It admits that our country is deeply affected by the war in Cuba and that its desires for peace are just. It declares that the present Spanish Government is bound by every consideration to a change of policy that should satisfy the United States and pacify Cuba within a reasonable time. To this end Spain has decided to put into effect the political reforms heretofore advocated by the present Premier, without halting for any consideration in the path which in its judgment leads to peace. The military operations, it is said, will continue but will be humane and conducted with all regard for private rights, being accompanied by political action leading to the autonomy of Cuba while guarding Spanish sovereignty. This, it is claimed, will result in investing Cuba with a distinct personality; the Island to be governed by an Executive and by a Local Council or Chamber, reserving to Spain the control of the foreign relations, the army and navy and the judicial administration. To accomplish this the present Government proposes to modify existing legislation by decree, leaving the Spanish Cortes, with the aid of Cuban Senators and Deputies, to solve the economic problem and properly distribute the existing debt. . . .

Throughout all these horrors and dangers to our own peace this Government has never in any way abrogated its sovereign prerogative of reserving to itself the determination of its policy and course according to its own high sense of right and in consonance with the dearest interests and convictions of our own people should the prolongation of the strife so demand.

Of the untried measures there remain only: Recognition of the Insurgents as belligerents; recognition of the independence of Cuba; neutral intervention to end the war by imposing a rational compromise between the contestants, and intervention in favor of one or the other party. I speak not of forcible annexation, for that can not be thought of. That by our code of morality would be criminal aggression.

Recognition of the belligerency of the Cuban insurgents has often been canvassed as a possible if not inevitable step both in regard to the previous ten years' struggle and during the present war. I am not unmindful that the two Houses of Congress in the spring of 1896 expressed the opinion by concurrent resolution that a condition of public war existed requiring or justifying the recognition of a state of belligerency in Cuba, and during the extra session the Senate voted a joint resolution of like import, which however was not brought to a vote in the House of Representatives. In the presence of these significant expressions of the sentiment of the Legislative branch it behooves the Executive to soberly consider the conditions under which so important a measure must needs rest for justification. It is to be seriously considered whether the Cuban insurrection possesses beyond dispute the attributes of Statehood which alone can demand the recognition of belligerency in its favor. Possession, in short, of the essential qualifications of sovereignty by the insurgents and the conduct of the war by them according to the received code of war are no less important factors toward the determination of the problem of belligerency than are the influences and consequences of the struggle upon the internal polity of the recognizing State. . . .

Turning to the practical aspects of a recognition of belligerency and reviewing its inconveniences and positive dangers, still further pertinent considerations appear. In the code of nations there is no such thing as a naked recognition of belligerency unaccompanied by the assumption of international neutrality. Such recognition without more will not confer upon either party to a domestic conflict a status not theretofore actually possessed or affect the relation of either party to other States. The act of recognition usually takes the form of a solemn proclamation of neutrality which recites the de facto condition of belligerency as its motive. It announces a domestic law of neutrality in the declaring State. It assumes the international obligations of a neutral in the presence of a public state of war. It warns all citizens and others within the jurisdiction of the proclaimant that they violate those rigorous obligations at their own peril and can not expect to be shielded from the consequences. The right of visit and search on the seas and seizure of vessels and cargoes and contraband of war and good prize under admiralty law must under international law be admitted as a legitimate consequence of a proclamation of belligerency. While according the equal belligerent rights defined by public law to each party in our ports disfavors would be imposed on both, which while nominally equal would weigh heavily in behalf of Spain herself. Possessing a navy and controlling the ports of Cuba her maritime rights could be asserted not only for the military investment of the Island but up to the margin of our own territorial waters, and a condition of things would exist for which the Cubans within their own domain could not hope to create a parallel; while its creation through aid or sympathy from within our domain would be even more impossible than now, with the additional obligations of international neutrality we would perforce assume.

The enforcement of this enlarged and onerous code of neutrality would only be influential within our own jurisdiction by land and sea and applicable by our own instrumentalities. It could impart to the United States no jurisdiction between Spain and the insurgents. It would give the United States no right of intervention to enforce the conduct of the strife within the paramount authority of Spain according to the international code of war.

For these reasons I regard the recognition of the belligerency of the Cuban insurgents as now unwise and therefore inadmissible. Should that step hereafter be deemed wise as a measure of right and duty the Executive will take it.

Intervention upon humanitarian grounds has been frequently suggested and has not failed to receive my most anxious and earnest consideration. But should such a step be now taken when it is apparent that a hopeful change has supervened in the policy of Spain toward Cuba? A new government has taken office in the mother country. It is pledged in advance to the declaration that all the effort in the world can not suffice to maintain peace in Cuba by the bayonet; that vague promises of reform after subjugation afford no solution of the insular problem; that with a substitution of commanders must come a change of the past system of warfare for one in harmony with a new policy which shall no longer aim to drive the Cubans to the "horrible alternative of taking to the thicket or succumbing in misery;" that reforms must be instituted in accordance with the needs and circumstances of the time, and that these reforms, while designed to give full autonomy to the colony and to create a virtual entity and self-controlled administration, shall yet conserve and affirm the sovereignty of Spain by a just distribution of powers and burdens upon a basis of mutual interest untainted by methods of selfish expediency.

The first acts of the new government lie in these honorable paths. The policy of cruel rapine and extermination that so long shocked the universal sentiment of humanity has been reversed. Under the new military commander a broad clemency is proffered. Measures have already been set on foot to relieve the horrors of starvation. The power of the Spanish armies it is asserted is to be used not to spread ruin and desolation but to protect the resumption of peaceful agricultural pursuits and productive industries. That past methods are futile to force a peace by subjugation is freely admitted, and that ruin without conciliation must inevitably fail to win for Spain the fidelity of a contented dependency.

Decrees in application of the foreshadowed reforms have already been promulgated. The full text of these decrees has not been received, but as furnished in a telegraphic summary from our Minister are: All civil and electoral rights of Peninsular Spaniards are, in virtue of existing constitutional authority, forthwith extended to Colonial Spaniards. A scheme of autonomy has been proclaimed by decree, to become effective upon ratification by the Cortes. It creates a Cuban parliament which, with the insular executive, can consider and vote upon all subjects affecting local order and interests, possessing unlimited powers save as to matters of state, war and the navy as to which the Governor-General acts by his own authority as the delegate of the central government. This parliament receives the oath of the Governor-General to preserve faithfully the liberties and privileges of the colony, and to it the colonial secretaries are responsible. It has the right to propose to the central government, through the Governor-General, modifications of the national charter and to invite new projects of law or executive measures in the interest of the colony.

Besides its local powers it is competent, first, to regulate electoral registration and procedure and prescribe the qualifications of electors and the manner of exercising suffrage; second, to organize courts of justice with native judges from members of the local bar; third, to frame the insular budget both as to expenditures and revenues, without limitation of any kind, and to set apart the revenues to meet the Cuban share of the national budget, which latter will be voted by the national Cortes with the assistance of Cuban senators and deputies; fourth, to initiate or take part in the negotiations of the national government for commercial treaties which may affect Cuban interests; fifth, to accept or reject commercial treaties which the national government may have concluded without the participation of the Cuban government; sixth, to frame the colonial tariff, acting in accord with the peninsular government in scheduling articles of mutual commerce between the mother country and the colonies. Before introducing or voting upon a bill, the Cuban government or the chambers will lay the project before the central government and hear its opinion thereon, all the correspondence in such regard being made public. Finally, all conflicts of jurisdiction arising between the different municipal, provincial and insular assemblies, or between the latter and the insular executive power, and which from their nature may not be referable to the central government for decision, shall be submitted to the courts.

That the Government of Sagasta has entered upon a course from which recession with honor is impossible can hardly be questioned; that in the few weeks it has existed it has made earnest of the sincerity of its professions is undeniable. I shall not impugn its sincerity, nor should impatience be suffered to embarrass it in the task it has undertaken. It is honestly due to Spain and to our friendly relations with Spain that she should be given a reasonable chance to realize her expectations and to prove the asserted efficacy of the new order of things to which she stands irrevocably committed. She has recalled the Commander whose brutal orders inflamed the American mind and shocked the civilized world. She has modified the horrible order of concentration and has undertaken to care for the helpless and permit those who desire to resume the cultivation of their fields to do so and assures them of the protection of the Spanish Government in their lawful occupations. She has just released the "Competitor" prisoners heretofore sentenced to death and who have been the subject of repeated diplomatic correspondence during both this and the preceding Administration.

Not a single American citizen is now in arrest or confinement in Cuba of whom this Government has any knowledge. The near future will demonstrate whether the indispensable condition of a righteous peace, just alike to the Cubans and to Spain as well as equitable to all our interests so intimately involved in the welfare of Cuba, is likely to be attained. If not, the exigency of further and other action by the United States will remain to be taken. When that time comes that action will be determined in the line of indisputable right and duty. It will be faced, without misgiving or hesitancy in the light of the obligation this Government owes to itself, to the people who have confided to it the protection of their interests and honor, and to humanity.

7   *Julius W. Pratt*
The Business Community Was Reluctant

Marxist ideologues, from Lenin to Herbert Aptheker, and career anti-imperialists such as J. A. Hobson, have denounced American expansion during this period as predicated on a lust for overseas markets and cheap sources of raw materials for further industrial exploitation of the masses. This thesis failed to gain any wide acceptance by historians, despite the charges leveled throughout the post-Versailles period that the bankers and industrialists (labeled in one book title as Merchants of Death) had led to American intervention in 1917 primarily for the sake of profits. In the midst of this controversy Julius W. Pratt published Expansionists of 1898 which, in effect, exonerated the business community as a, much less the, causal factor in promoting war with Spain in 1898. Does his analysis of press and public opinion during this period support a "psychic crisis" or a "jingo" journalism thesis in explaining the advent of war?

American business, in general, had strongly opposed action that would lead to war with Spain. American business had been either opposed or indifferent to the expansionist philosophy which had arisen since 1890. But almost at the moment when the war began, a large section of American business had, for reasons that will become apparent, been converted to the belief that a program of territorial expansion would serve its purposes. Hence business, in the end, welcomed the "large policy" and

SOURCE. Julius W. Pratt, *Expansionists of 1898: The Acquisition of Hawaii and the Spanish Islands,* Baltimore: The Johns Hopkins Press, 1936, pp. 233–257 *passim.* Reprinted by permission of the publisher and the author.

exerted its share of pressure for the retention of the Spanish islands and such related policies as the annexation of Hawaii and the construction of an isthmian canal.

One public man to whom the welfare of American business was of so much concern that he may almost be considered its spokesman in the Senate, was McKinley's friend, Mark Hanna. No one was more unwilling than he to see the United States drift into war with Spain. To Hanna, in the words of his biographer, "the outbreak of war seemed to imperil the whole policy of domestic economic amelioration which he placed before every other object of political action." Hanna's attitude appears to have been identical with that of leading business men. This conclusion is based not only upon the few published biographies of such men, but also upon the study of a large number of financial and trade periodicals, of the proceedings of chambers of commerce and boards of trade, and of material in the *Miscellaneous Files* of the Department of State, containing numerous letters and petitions from business men and organizations.

That business sentiment, especially in the East, was strongly anti-war at the close of 1897 and in the opening months of 1898, is hardly open to doubt. Wall Street stocks turned downward whenever the day's news seemed to presage war and climbed again with information favorable to peace. Bulls and bears on the market were those who anticipated, respectively, a peaceable and a warlike solution of the Cuban question. The "jingo," in Congress or the press, was an object of intense dislike to the editors of business and financial journals, who sought to counteract his influence by anti-war editorials in their columns. Boards of trade and chambers of commerce added their pleas for the maintenance of peace to those of the business newspapers and magazines. So marked, indeed, was the anti-war solidarity of the financial interests and their spokesmen that the jingoes fell to charging Wall Street with want of patriotism. Wall Street, declared the Sacramento *Evening Bee* (March 11, 1898), was "the colossal and aggregate Benedict Arnold of the Union, and the syndicated Judas Iscariot of humanity." Senator Thurston, of Nebraska, charged that opposition to war was found only among the "money-changers," bringing from the editor of *The American*

Banker the reply that "there is not an intelligent, self-respecting and civilized American citizen anywhere who would not prefer to have the existing crisis culminate in peaceful negotiations."

This anti-war attitude on the part of several leading financial journals continued up to the very beginning of hostilities. . . .

The reasons for this attitude on the part of business are not far to seek. Since the panic of 1893 American business had been in the doldrums. Tendencies toward industrial revival had been checked, first by the Venezuela war scare in December, 1895, and again by the free silver menace in 1896. But in 1897 began a real revival, and before the end of the year signs of prosperity appeared on all sides. The New York *Commercial* conducted a survey of business conditions in a wide variety of trades and industries, from which it concluded that, "after three years of waiting and of false starts, the groundswell of demand has at last begun to rise with a steadiness which leaves little doubt that an era of prosperity has appeared." January, 1898, said the same article, is "a supreme moment in the period of transition from depression to comparative prosperity." This note of optimism one meets at every turn, even in such a careful and conservative sheet as the *Commercial and Financial Chronicle.* As early as July, 1897, this paper remarked: "We appear to be on the eve of a revival in business"; and in December after remarking upon the healthy condition of the railroads and the iron industry, it concluded: "In brief, no one can study the industrial conditions of today in America without a feeling of elation. . . ." The *Wall Street Journal* found only two "blue spots" in the entire country: Boston, which suffered from the depressed demand for cotton goods, and New York, where senseless rate cutting by certain railroads caused uneasiness. "Throughout the west, southwest and on the Pacific coast business has never been better, nor the people more hopeful."

A potent cause for optimism was found in the striking expansion of the American export trade. A volume of exports far in excess of those of any recent year, a favorable balance of trade of $286,000,000, and an especially notable increase in exports of manufactures of iron, steel, and copper, convinced practically every business expert that the United States was on the point of capturing the markets of the world. "There is no question," said one journal, "that the world, generally, is looking more and more to the United States as the source of its supply for very many of the staple commodities of life." Especially elated were spokesmen of the iron and steel industry. Cheaper materials and improved methods were enabling the American producer to undersell his British competitor in Europe and in the British possessions, and Andrew Carnegie was talking of a great shipbuilding yard near New York to take advantage of these low costs. The *Iron Age,* in an editorial on "The Future of Business," foretold the abolition of the business cycle by means of a better planned economy, consolidation of railroads and industries, reduction of margins of profit, higher wages, and lower prices to consumers.

To this fair prospect of a great business revival the threat of war was like a spectre at the feast. A foreign complication, thought the *Commercial and Financial Chronicle* in October, 1897, would quickly mar "the trade prosperity which all are enjoying." Six months later (April 2, 1898), after a discussion of the effect of war rumors on the stock exchange, it declared: " . . . Every influence has been, and even now is, tending strongly towards a term of decided prosperity, and that the Cuban disturbance, and it alone, has arrested the movement and checked enterprise." The *Banker and Tradesman* saw in the Cuban complication the threat of a "material setback to the prosperous conditions which had just set in after five years of panic and depression." The same journal summarized a calculation made by the Boston *Transcript* showing that in February, 1898, the wave of prosperity had carried the average price of twenty-five leading stocks within $5\frac{1}{2}$ points of the high for the preceding ten years and 30 points above the low of 1896, and that the Cuban trouble had, in a little over two months, caused a loss of over ten points, or more than one-third of the recent gain. "War would impede the march of prosperity and put the country back many years," said the *New Jersey Trade Review.* The *Railway Age* was of the opinion that the country was coming out of a depression and needed peace to complete its recovery. "From a commercial and mercenary standpoint," it remarked, "it seems peculiarly bitter that this war should have come when the country had already suffered so much and so needed rest and peace."

The idea that war could bring any substantial benefits to business was generally scouted. It would endanger our currency stability, interrupt our trade, and threaten our coasts and our commerce, thought the *Commercial and Financial Chronicle*. It would "incalculably increase the loss to business interests," said the *Banker's Magazine;* while the *United States Investor* held that war was "never beneficial from a material standpoint, that is, in the long run." The *Railroad Gazette* predicted that war would result in the "interruption of business enterprise of every kind, stopping new projects and diminution of the output of existing businesses and contraction of trade everywhere." Railroads would lose more than they would gain. Even arms manufacturers were not all agreed that war would be desirable. Journals speaking for the iron and steel industry also argued that war would injure business. It "would injure the iron and steel makers ten times as much as they would be benefited by the prevailing spurt in the manufacture of small arms, projectiles and steel plates for war ships," in the opinion of one of these. The *American Wool and Cotton Reporter* of New York and the *Northwestern Miller* of Minneapolis agreed that war was never materially beneficial in the long run, while trade journals in Atlanta, Chattanooga, and Portland, Oregon, saw as fruits of the approaching conflict only destruction, debt, and depressed industry.

Many conservative interests feared war for the specific reason that it might derange the currency and even revive the free-silver agitation, which had seemed happily dead. The subsidence of that agitation and the prospect of currency reform were among the hopeful factors at the close of 1897. It was not uncommonly charged that the jingoes were animated in part by the expectation that war would lead to inflation in paper or silver. . . .

Something of a freak among New York financial journals was the *Financial Record,* which, in November, 1897, denounced "the cowardice of our Administration in refusing the phenomenally brave Cubans the commonest rights of belligerency" as "a disgrace to the United States," and argued that war with Spain, far from depressing securities or injuring business, "would vastly increase the net earning power of every security sold on our market today." The mystery of this jingo attitude is explained when we discover that this journal had been a warm advocate of the free coinage of silver.

Business opinion in the West, especially in the Mississippi Valley, appears to have been less opposed to war and less apprehensive of its results than that of the Atlantic coast. The Kansas City Board of Trade, at the beginning of 1897, had urged recognition of Cuban independence. The Cincinnati Chamber of Commerce, at a meeting on March 29, 1898, adopted "amidst much enthusiasm" resolutions condemning Spain for cruelties to the Cubans and the destruction of the "Maine" and calling for a "firm and vigorous policy which will have for its purpose— peacefully if we can, but with force if we must—the redress of past wrongs, and the complete and unqualified independence of Cuba." The Chicago *Economist* denied that war would seriously hurt business or endanger the gold standard and asserted that the liberation of Cuba, by peace or war, would mean another star of glory for the United States and would produce "results of the highest value to mankind." The *Rand-McNally Bankers' Monthly*, of the same city, while opposing war, called attention to the fact that while the war scare had demoralized the stock market, "general business activity apparently received an impetus." Similarly the *Age of Steel* (St. Louis), while much preferring peace, "when not secured at the price of national honor," comforted its readers with the thought that although foreign trade might suffer, home trade and industries would be stimulated by war. . . . The *Mining and Scientific Press,* of San Francisco, while holding that, in general, war "lets loose havoc and waste, and entails destructive expense," conceded that "to nearly everything related to the mining industry the war will be a stimulus."

Even in New York, business men saw some rays of light piercing the war clouds. Stock market operators, according to the *Wall Street Journal,* just after the "Maine" explosion, "did not look for any great break in the market, because actual war with Spain would be a very small affair compared with the Venezuela complication with Great Britain." Their expectation was for a drop in stocks at the beginning of hostilities, followed by a resumption of the recent advance. In fact, the first shock might well be followed by a boom. "The nation looks for peace," declared *Dun's Review,* March 5, "but knows that its sources of prosperity are quite beyond the reach of any attack that is possible." *Bradstreet's* contrasted the jumpiness of Wall Street over war news with "the calm way in which general business interests have regarded the current foreign complications," and *Dun's Review* of March 12 stated that no industry or branch of business showed any restriction, while some had been rapidly gaining, that railroads were increasing their profits while speculators sold their stocks, and that there was a growing demand for the products of all the great industries.

Despite such expressions as these, there seems little reason to question the belief that an overwhelming preponderance of the vocal business interests of the country strongly desired peace. By the middle of March, however, many organs of business opinion were admitting that a war with Spain might bring no serious disaster, and there was a growing conviction that such a war was inevitable. In the Senate on March 17, Senator Redfield Proctor, of Vermont, described, from his own observation, the terrible sufferings of the Cuban "reconcentrados." Proctor was supposedly no sensationalist, and his speech carried great weight. The *Wall Street Journal* described its effect among the denizens of the Street. "Senator Proctor's speech," it said, "converted a great many people in Wall Street, who have heretofore taken the ground that the United States has no business to interfere in a revolution on Spanish soil. These men had been among the most prominent in deploring the whole Cuban matter, but there was no question about the accuracy of Senator Proctor's statements and as many of them expressed it, they made the blood boil." The *American Banker,* hitherto a firm opponent of intervention, remarked on March 23 that Proctor's speech showed an intolerable state of things, in view of which it could not understand "how any one with a grain of human sympathy within him can dispute the propriety of a policy of intervention, so only that this outraged people might be set free!" It still hoped, however, for a peaceful solution, declaring that the United States ought to urge the Cubans to accept the Spanish offer of autonomy. That this growing conviction that something must be done about Cuba was by no means equivalent to a desire for war, was clearly revealed a few days later. Rumors circulated to the effect that Spain was willing to sell Cuba and that J. P. Morgan's return from a trip abroad was connected with plans to finance the purchase. "There is much satisfaction expressed in Wall Street," said the *Wall Street Journal*, "at the prospects of having Cuba free, because it is believed that this will take one of the most disturbing factors out of the situation. . . . Even if $200,000,000 is the indemnity demanded it is a sum which the United States could well afford to pay to get rid of the trouble." Even $250,-000,000, it was thought, would be insignificant in comparison with the probable cost of a war.

It remains to examine the attitude of certain American business men and corporations having an immediate stake in Cuba, or otherwise liable to be directly affected by American intervention. Much American capital, as is well known, was invested in the Cuban sugar industry. Upon this industry the civil war fell with peculiarly devastating effect, not only cutting off profits on capital so invested, but also crippling a valuable carrying trade between Cuba and the United States. Naturally enough, some firms suffering under these conditions desired to see the United States intervene to end the war, though such intervention might lead to war between the United States and Spain. In May, 1897, a memorial on the subject bearing over three hundred signatures was presented to John Sherman, Secretary of State. The signers described themselves as "citizens of the United States, doing business as bankers, merchants, manufacturers, steamship owners and agents in the cities of Boston, New York, Philadelphia, Baltimore, Savannah, Charleston, Jacksonville, New Orleans, and other places, and also other citizens of the United States, who have been for many years engaged in the export and import trade with the Island of Cuba." They called attention to the serious losses to which their businesses had been subjected by the hostilities in Cuba and expressed the hope that, in order to prevent further loss, to reestablish American commerce, and also to secure "the blessings of peace for one and a half millions of residents of the Island of Cuba now enduring unspeakable distress and suffering," the United States Government might take steps to bring about an honorable reconciliation between the parties to the conflict.

Another memorial, signed by many of the same subscribers, was presented to President McKinley on February 9, 1898, by a committee of New York business men. It asserted that the Cuban war, which had now continued for three entire years, had caused an average loss of $100,000,000 a year, or a total loss of $300,-000,000 in the import and export trade between Cuba and the United States, to which were to be added "heavy sums irretrievably lost by the destruction of American properties, or properties supported by American capital in the Island itself, such as sugar factories, railways, tobacco plantations, mines and other industrial enterprises; the loss of the United States in trade and capital by means of this war being probably far greater and more serious than that of all the other parties concerned, not excepting Spain herself."

The sugar crop of 1897–1898, continued the memorial, appeared for the most part lost like its two predecessors, and unless peace could be established before May or June of the current year, the crop of 1898–1899, with all the business dependent upon it, would likewise be lost, since the rainy season of summer and fall would be required "to prepare for next winter's crop, by repairing damaged fields, machinery, lines of railways, &c." In view of the importance to the United States of the Cuban trade and of American participation "in the ownership or management of Cuban sugar factories, railways and other enterprises," the petitioners hoped that the President would deem the situation "of sufficient importance as to warrant prompt and efficient measures by our Government, with the sole object of restoring peace . . . and with it restoring to us a most valuable commercial field."

How much weight such pressure from special interests had with the administration there is no way of knowing. But it is to be noted that the pressure from parties directly interested was not all on one side. Mr. E. F. Atkins, an American citizen who divided his time between Boston and his sugar plantation of Soledad near Cienfuegos, Cuba, which he had developed at a cost of $1,400,000, had been able, through protection received from the Spanish Government and through a corps of guards organized and paid by himself, to continue operations throughout the period of the insurrection. He was frequently in Washington, where he had influential friends, during both the Cleveland and McKinley administrations and worked consistently against the adoption of any measures likely to provoke war.

Unlike some of the sugar plantations, American-owned iron mines in Cuba continued to do active business despite the insurrection. Three American iron and manganese enterprises in the single province of Santiago claimed to have an investment of some $6,000,000 of purely American capital, a large portion of which was in property which could easily be destroyed. "We are fully advised as to our status in case of war," wrote the representative of one company to the Assistant Secretary of State, "and that this property might be subject to confiscation or destruction by the Spanish Government." War between Spain and the United States, wrote the president of another company, "will very likely mean the destruction of our valuable plant and in any event untold loss to our Company and its American stockholders." An American cork company with large interests in Spain; a New York merchant with trade in the Mediterranean and Black Sea; a Mobile firm which had chartered a Spanish ship to carry a cargo of timber—these are samples of American business interests which saw in war the threat of direct damage to themselves. . . .

It seems safe to conclude, from the evidence available, that the only important business interests (other than the business of sensational journalism) which clamored for intervention in Cuba were those directly or indirectly concerned in the Cuban sugar industry; that opposed to intervention were the influence of other parties (including at least one prominent sugar planter) whose business would suffer direct injury from war and also the overwhelming preponderance of general business opinion. After the middle of March, 1898, some conservative editors came to think intervention inevitable on humanitarian grounds, but many of the most influential business journals opposed it to the end.

We can now turn to the question whether American business was imperialistic; whether, in other words, business opinion favored schemes for acquiring foreign territory to supply it with markets, fields for capital investment, or commercial and naval stations in distant parts of the world. American business men were not unaware of the struggle for colonies then raging among European nations. Did they feel that the United States ought to participate in that struggle?

The rising tide of prosperity was intimately connected with the increase in American exports, particularly of manufactured articles. That the future welfare of American industry was dependent upon the command of foreign markets was an opinion so common as to appear almost universal. The New York *Journal of Commerce* pointed out, early in 1897, that the nation's industrial plant had been developed far beyond the needs of domestic consumption. In the wire nail industry there was said to be machinery to make four times as many nails as the American markets could consume. Rail mills, locomotive shops, and glass factories were in a similar situation. "Nature has thus destined this country for the industrial supremacy of the world," said the same paper later in the year. When the National Association of Manufacturers met in New York for its annual convention in January, 1898, "the discussion of ways and means for extending this country's trade, and more particularly its export business, was, in fact, almost the single theme of the speakers," according to *Bradstreet's,* which added the comment: "Nothing is more significant of the changed attitude toward this country's foreign trade, manifested by the American manufacturer today as compared with a few years ago, than the almost single devotion which he pays to the subject of possible export-trade extension."

But if business men believed, prior to the opening of the war with Spain, that foreign markets were to be secured through the acquisition of colonies, they were strangely silent about it. To the program of colonial expansion which for almost a decade had been urged by such men as Mahan, Albert Shaw, Lodge, Roosevelt, and Morgan, business had remained, to all appearances, either indifferent or antagonistic. To the business man, such a program was merely one form of dangerous jingoism. A large section of business opinion had, indeed, favored plans for the building of a Nicaraguan canal with governmental assistance, and some spokesmen for business had favored annexation of the Hawaiian Islands. But beyond these relatively modest projects few business men, apparently, wished to go. Two of the most important commercial journals, the New York *Journal of Commerce* and the *Commercial and Financial Chronicle,* had stoutly opposed both the canal scheme and Hawaiian annexation. The former satirized the arguments of the proponents of both schemes. "We must certainly build the canal to defend the islands, and it is quite clear that we must acquire the islands . . . in order to defend the canal." The canal was not only unnecessary, but unless fortified at each end and patrolled by two fleets, it would be a positive misfortune. Such protection—"the price of jingoism"— might "easily cost us $25,000,000 a year, besides the lump sum that will be required for the original investment, and there is absolutely no excuse whatever in our commercial or our political interests for a single step in this long procession of expenses and of complications with foreign powers." As for Hawaii and Cuba, neither was fit for self-government as a state,—and the American constitution provided no machinery for governing dependencies. The Hawaiian Islands would have no military value unless the United States were to build a great navy and take an aggressive attitude in the Pacific. The *Commercial and Financial Chronicle* saw in colonies only useless outposts which must be protected at great expense, and the St. Louis *Age of Steel* warned lest the expansion of the export trade might "lead to territorial greed, as in the case of older nations, the price of which in armaments and militarism offsets the gain made by the spindle and the forge."

Colonies were not only certain to bear a fruit of danger and expense; they were valueless from the commercial point of view. Did not the colonies of Great Britain afford us one of the most valuable of our export markets? Did we not trade as advantageously with Guiana, a British colony, as with independent Venezuela? "Most of our ideas of the commercial value of conquests, the commercial uses of navies and the commercial advantages of political control," said the New York *Journal of Commerce,* dated back to times when colonial policies were designed to monopolize colonial trade for the mother country. The *Commercial and Financial Chronicle* believed that the current European enthusiasm for colonies was based on false premises; for although trade often followed the flag, "the trade is not always with the home markets of the colonizer. England and the United States are quite as apt to slip in with their wares under the very Custom-House pennant of the French or German dependency." Outright opposition, such as this, to the idea of colonial expansion is not common in the business periodicals examined; much more common is complete silence on the subject. Positive and negative evidence together seem to warrant the conclusion that American business in general, at the opening of 1898, was either indifferent to imperialism, or definitely opposed.

8   *Walter LaFeber*

The Business Community was the Most Influential Lobby for War

Educated at the graduate schools of Stanford and Wisconsin (Ph.D. 1959), where he studied under Thomas A. Bailey, Fred Harvey Harrington, and William A. Williams, Walter LaFeber (1933–   ) is now one of America's most respected historians and teachers. His first book, The New Empire, won the Beveridge Prize in 1963. Here he challenged the Pratt arguments on two mjaor points; viz., the role of business as a motivating factor in bringing on war with Spain, and the leadership role of McKinley in effecting a consciously planned Cuban policy in accordance with the wishes of the business community. In this selection note his repeated use of qualifying adjectives and adverbs. Does this

SOURCE. Reprinted from Walter LaFeber; *The New Empire: An Interpretation of American Expansion, 1860–1898,* pp. 385–387, 390–391, and 397–406. Copyright 1963 by the American Historical Association. Used by permission of Cornell University Press and the author.

imply that the matter is still open to further investigation and re-assessment?

The American business community was by no means monolithic in its opposition to war. To say as a generalization that business-men opposed war is as erroneous as saying that businessmen wanted war. It is possible to suggest, however, that by the middle of March (1898) important businessmen and spokesmen for the business community were advocating war. It is also possible to suggest that at the same time, a shift seemed to be occurring in the general business community regarding its over-all views on the desirability of war.

Financial journals which advocated bimetallism had long urged a stronger attitude toward Spain in the hope that the resulting conflict would force the Treasury to pay expenses in silver. More important, business spokesmen in such midwestern and western cities as Cincinnati, Louisville, St. Louis, Chicago, San Francisco, and especially Pittsburgh were not reluctant to admit that they would welcome war. . . .

A strong possibility exists that the antiwar commercial journals in New York spoke for the less important members of that financial community. Russell Sage, claiming that he spoke "not only my own views on this point, but those of other moneyed men with whom I have talked," demanded that if the "Maine" was blown up by an outside force "the time for action has come. There should be no wavering." If war did occur, "There is no question as to where the rich men stand"; they would buy govern-ment bonds as they had during the Civil War and do all in their power to bolster the nation's war resources. W. C. Beer, who attempted to make a thorough survey of leading businessmen's opinion, concluded that "the steady opponents of the war among financiers were simply the life insurance men and small bankers." Beer found such giants as John Jacob Astor, John Gates, Thomas Fortune Ryan, William Rockefeller, and Stuyvesant Fish "feeling militant." On March 28 J. Pierpont Morgan declared that further talk of arbitration would accomplish nothing. . . .

Perhaps the American business community exerted the most

influence on the administration during the last two weeks in March when influential business spokesmen began to welcome the possibility of war in order to end the suspense which shrouded the commercial exchanges. Although other historians have touched briefly on this important change, it should be noted that some important business spokesmen and President McKinley apparently arrived at this decision at approximately the same time.

During the first two months of 1898 the United States began to enjoy prosperous conditions for the first time in five years. The de Lôme and "Maine" incidents affected business conditions only in the stock exchanges, and even there the impact was slight. Business improved, especially in the West and Northwest. In early March very few business journals feared a return of depression conditions, and with the gold influx resulting from discoveries in Alaska and from the export surplus, even fewer business observers displayed anxiety over the silver threat.

But in mid-March financial reporters noted that business in commodities as well as stocks had suddenly slowed. Henry Clay Frick had been optimistic in his business reports to Andrew Carnegie, who was vacationing in Scotland. But on March 24, Frick reported that "owing to uncertainty . . . of the Cuban trouble, business is rather stagnant." A Wall Street correspondent wrote on March 22 that "the last two days have been the dullest for many a month." On March 26 the *Commercial and Financial Chronicle* summarized the situation. No "sudden and violent drop in prices" had occurred. But the rapid progress in trade had stopped and now "frequent complaints are heard. The volume of trade undoubtedly remains large, but the reports speak of new enterprises being held in check."

Businessmen had been particularly influenced by the speech of Senator Redfield Proctor of Vermont on March 17. Proctor was known for his conservative, antiwar disposition, an attitude he shared with his intimate friend, William McKinley. But the Senator had just returned from a visit to Cuba, a visit that had profoundly shocked him. Proctor discounted Spanish reforms as "too late," but he advised against going to war over the "Maine." The United States should use force, Proctor intimated, only to deliver the Cuban people from "the worst misgovernment of which I ever had knowledge." Conversations with businessmen in Cuba had provided him with most of his information; these men had declared "without exception" that it was too late for any more schemes of autonomy. They wanted an American protectorate, annexation, or a free Cuba. Although Proctor did not say so explicitly, none of these solutions was immediately possible without war with Spain. This speech deeply impressed almost all of the conservative and business journals which had opposed war. Many of these journals did not overlook Proctor's role as one of McKinley's "most trusted advisors and friends." Two weeks later the New York *Commercial Advertiser* looked back and marked this speech as the turning point in the road to war. . . .

McKinley had had the choice of three policies which would have terminated the Cuban revolution. First, he could have let the Spanish forces and the insurgents fight until one or the other fell exhausted from the bloodshed and financial strain. During the struggle the United States could have administered food and medicine to the civilian population, a privilege which the Spanish agreed to allow in March, 1898. Second, the President could have demanded an armistice and Spanish assurances that negotiations over the summer would result in some solution which would pacify American feelings. That is to say, he could have followed Woodford's ideas. Third, McKinley could have demanded both an armistice and Spanish assurances that Cuba would become independent immediately. If Spain would not grant both of these conditions, American military intervention would result. The last was the course the President followed.

Each of these policy alternatives deserves a short analysis. For American policy makers, the first choice was the least acceptable of the three, but the United States did have to deal, nevertheless, with certain aspects of this policy. If Spain hoped to win such a conflict, she had to use both the carrot of an improved and attractive autonomy scheme and the stick of an increased and effective military force. Spain could have granted no amount of autonomy, short of complete independence, which would have satisfied the rebels, and whether Americans cared to admit it or not, they were at least partially responsible for this obstinancy on the part of the insurgents. The United States did attempt to stop filibustering expeditions, but a large number nevertheless reached Cuban shores. More important, when the Spanish Minister asked Day to disband the New York Junta, the financial taproot of the insurgent organization, the Assistant Secretary replied that "this was not possible under American law and in the present state of public feeling." Woodford had given the Spanish Queen the same reply in mid-January. It was perhaps at this point that Spain saw the last hopes for a negotiated peace begin to flicker away.

Seemingly unrelated actions by the United States gave boosts to the rebel cause. The sending of the "Maine," for instance, considerably heartened the rebels; they believed that the warship diverted Spanish attention and military power from insurgent forces. When the vessel exploded, the New York Junta released a statement which did not mourn the dead sailors as much as it mourned the sudden disappearance of American power in Havana harbor. The Junta interpreted the passage of the $50,000,000 war appropriation measure during the first week of March as meaning either immediate war or the preparation for war. Under such conditions, it was not odd that the rebels were reluctant to compromise their objective of complete independence.

If the insurgents would not have accepted autonomy, no matter how liberal or attractive, then Spain might have hoped to suppress the rebels with outright force. To have done so, however, the Spanish government would have had to bring its army through the rainy season with few impairments, resume to a large extent the *reconcentrado* policies, and prevent all United States aid from reaching the rebels. The first objective would have been difficult, but the last two, if carried out, would have meant war with the United States. The State Department could not allow Spain to reimpose methods even faintly resembling Weyler's techniques, nor could the Department have allowed the searching of American vessels. McKinley and the American people hoped that Spain would stop the revolution, but they also insisted on taking from Spain the only tools with which that nation could deal with the Cubans.

Having found this first alternative impossible to accept, Mc-Kinley might have chosen a second approach: demand an armistice and ultimate pacification of the island, but attempt to achieve this peacefully over several months and with due respect for the sovereignty of Spain. This was the alternative Woodford hoped the administration would choose. He had reported during the two weeks before McKinley's message that the Spanish had given in time and time again on points which he had believed they could not afford to grant. In spite of the threat of revolution from the army, the Queen had granted a temporary truce. The American Minister continued to ask for more time to find a peaceful settlement. On April 11, the day the war message went to Congress, Woodford wrote the President, "To-day it is just possible that Moret and I have been right (in our pursuit of peace), but it is too soon to be jubilant." The American Minister sincerely believed that the negotiations during the period of truce could, with good faith on both the American and Spanish sides, result in Spain evacuating the island. This would have to be done slowly, however. No sovereign nation could be threatened with a time limit and uncompromising demands without fighting back. The fact that Spain would not grant McKinley's demand for immediate Cuban independence makes the Spanish-American War which began in April, 1898, by no means an inevitable conflict. Any conflict is inevitable once one proud and sovereign power, dealing with a similar power, decides to abandon the conference table and issue an ultimatum. The historical problem remains: which power took the initiative in setting the conditions that   resulted in armed conflict, and were those conditions justified?

By April 10 McKinley had assumed an inflexible position. The President abjured this second alternative and demanded not only a truce, but a truce which would lead to a guarantee of immediate Cuban independence obtained with the aid of American mediation. He moreover demanded such a guarantee of independence before the Cortes or the Cuban parliament, the two groups which had the constitutional power to grant such independence, were to gather for their formal sessions.

The central question is, of course, why McKinley found himself in such a position on April 10 that only the third alternative was open to him. The President did not want war; he had been sincere and tireless in his efforts to maintain the peace. By mid-March, however, he was beginning to discover that, although he did not want war, he did want what only a war could provide: the disappearance of the terrible uncertainty in American political and economic life, and a solid basis from which to resume the building of the new American commercial empire. When the President made his demands, therefore, he made the ultimate demands; as far as he was concerned, a six-month period of negotiations would not serve to temper the political and economic problems in the United States, but only exacerbate them.

To say this is to raise another question: why did McKinley arrive at this position during mid-March? What were the factors which limited the President's freedom of choice and policies at this particular time? The standard interpretations of the war's causes emphasize the yellow journals and a belligerent Congress. These were doubtlessly crucial factors in shaping the course of American entry into the conflict, but they must be used carefully. A first observation should be that Congress and the yellow press, which had been loudly urging intervention ever since 1895, did not make a maiden appearance in March, 1898; new elements had to enter the scene at that time to act as the catalysts for McKinley's policy. Other facts should be noted regarding the yellow press specifically. In areas where this press supposedly was most important, such as New York City, no more than one-third of the press could be considered sensational. The strongest and most widespread prowar journalism apparently occurred in the Midwest. But there were few yellow journals there. The papers that advocated war in this section did so for reasons other than sensationalism; among these reasons were the influence of the Cuban Junta and, perhaps most important, the belief that the United States possessed important interests in the Caribbean area which had to be protected. Finally, the yellow press obviously did not control the levers of American foreign policy. McKinley held these, and he bitterly attacked the owners of the sensational journals as "evil disposed . . .people." An interpretation stressing rabid journalism as a major cause of the war should draw some link to illustrate how these journals reached the White House or the State Department. To say that this influence was exerted through public opinion proves nothing; the next problem is to demonstrate how much public opinion was governed by the yellow press, how much of this opinion was influenced by more sober factors, and which of these two branches of opinion most influenced McKinley.

Congress was a hotbed of interventionist sentiment, but then it had been so since 1895. The fact was that Congress had more trouble handling McKinley than the President had handling Congress. The President had no fear of that body. He told Charles Dawes during the critical days of February and March that if Congress tried to adjourn he would call it back into session. McKinley held Congress under control until the last two days of March, when the publication of the "Maine" investigation forced Thomas B. Reed, the passionately antiwar Speaker of the House, to surrender to the onslaughts of the rapidly increasing interventionist forces. As militants in Congress forced the moderates into full retreat, McKinley and Day were waiting in the White House for Spain's reply to the American ultimatum. And after the outbreak on March 31 McKinley reassumed control. On April 5 the Secretary of War, R. A. Alger, assured the President that several important senators had just informed him that "there will be no trouble about holding the Senate." When the President postponed his war message on April 5 in order to grant Fitzhugh Lee's request for more time, prowar congressmen went into a frenzy. During the weekend of April 8 and 9, they condemned the President, ridiculed Reed's impotence to hold back war, and threatened to declare war themselves. In fact, they did nearly everything except disobey McKinley's wishes that nothing be done until the following week. Nothing was done.

When the Senate threatened to overrule the President's orders that the war declaration exclude recognition of the Cuban insurgent government, McKinley whipped the doubters into line and forced the Senate to recede from its position. This was an all-out battle between the White House and a strong Senate faction. McKinley triumphed despite extremely strong pressure exerted by sincere American sentiment on behalf of immediate Cuban independence and despite the more crass material interests of the Junta's financial supporters and spokesmen. The President wanted to have a free hand in dealing with Cuba after the war, and Congress granted his wishes. Events on Capitol Hill may have been more colorful than those at the White House, but the latter, not the former, was the center of power in March and April, 1898.

Influences other than the yellow press or congressional belligerence were more important in shaping McKinley's position of April 11. Perhaps most important was the transformation of the opinion of many spokesmen for the business community who had formerly opposed war. If, as one journal declared, the McKinley administration, "more than any that have preceded it, sustains . . . close relations to the business interests of the country," then this change of business sentiment should not be discounted. This transformation brought important financial spokesmen, especially from the Northeast, into much the same position that had long been occupied by prointerventionist business groups and journals in the trans-Appalachian area. McKinley's decision to intervene placated many of the same business spokesmen whom he had satisfied throughout 1897 and January and February of 1898 by his refusal to declare war.

Five factors may be delineated which shaped this interventionist sentiment of the business community. First, some business journals emphasized the material advantages to be gained should Cuba become a part of the world in which the United States would enjoy, in the words of the New York *Commercial Advertiser*, "full freedom of development in the whole world's interest." The *Banker's Magazine* noted that "so many of our citizens are so involved in the commerce and productions of the island, that to protect these interests . . . the United States will have eventually to force the establishment of fair and reasonable government." The material damage suffered by investors in Cuba and by many merchants, manufacturers, exporters, and importers, as, for example, the groups which presented the February 10 petition to McKinley, forced these interests to advocate a solution which could be obtained only through force.

A second reason was the uncertainty that plagued the business community in mid-March. This uncertainty was increased by Proctor's powerful and influential speech and by the news that a Spanish torpedo-boat flotilla was sailing from Cadiz to Cuba. The uncertainty was exemplified by the sudden stagnation of trade on the New York Stock Exchange after March 17. Such an unpredictable economic basis could not provide the spring-board for the type of overseas commercial empire that McKinley and numerous business spokesmen envisioned.

Third, by March many businessmen who had deprecated war on the ground that the United States Treasury did not possess adequate gold reserves began to realize that they had been arguing from false assumptions. The heavy exports of 1897 and the dis-coveries of gold in Alaska and Australia brought the yellow metal into the country in an ever widening stream. Private bankers had been preparing for war since 1897. *Banker's Magazine* sum-marized these developments: "Therefore, while not desiring war, it is apparent that the country now has an ample coin basis for sustaining the credit operations which a conflict would probably make necessary. In such a crisis the gold standard will prove a bulwark of confidence."

Fourth, antiwar sentiment lost much strength when the nation realized that it had nothing to fear from European intervention on the side of Spain. France and Russia, who were most sympa-thetic to the Spanish monarchy, were forced to devote their attention to the Far East. Neither of these nations wished to alienate the United States on the Cuban issue. More important, Americans happily realized that they had the support of Great Britain. The *rapprochement* which had occurred since the Venezuelan incident now paid dividends. On an official level, the British Foreign Office assured the State Department that nothing would be accomplished in the way of European inter-vention unless the United States requested such intervention. The British attitude made it easy for McKinley to deal with a joint European note of April 6 which asked for American moderation toward Spain. The President brushed off the request firmly but politely. On an unofficial level, American periodicals expressed appreciation of the British policy on Cuba, and some of the journals noted that a common Anglo-American approach was also desirable in Asia. The European reaction is interesting insofar as it evinces the continental powers' growing realization that the United States was rapidly becoming a major force in the world. But the European governments set no limits on American dealings with Spain. McKinley could take the initiative and make his demands with little concern for European reactions.

Finally, opposition to war melted away in some degree when the administration began to emphasize that the United States enjoyed military power much superior to that of Spain. One possible reason for McKinley's policies during the first two months of 1898 might have been his fear that the nation was not adequately prepared. As late as the weekend of March 25 the President worried over this inadequacy. But in late February and early March, especially after the $50,000,000 appropriation by Congress, the country's military strength developed rapidly. On March 13 the Philadelphia *Press* proclaimed that American naval power greatly exceeded that of the Spanish forces. By early April those who feared a Spanish bombardment of New York City were in the small minority. More representative were the views of Winthrop Chanler who wrote Lodge that if Spanish troops invaded New York "they would all be absorbed in the population . . . and engaged in selling oranges before they got as far as 14th Street."

As the words of McKinley's war message flew across the wires to Madrid, many business spokesmen who had opposed war had recently changed their minds, American military forces were rapidly growing more powerful, banks and the United States Treasury had secured themselves against the initial shocks of war, and the European powers were divided among themselves and preoccupied in the Far East. Business boomed after McKinley signed the declaration of war. "With a hesitation so slight as to amount almost to indifference," *Bradstreet's* reported on April 30, "the business community, relieved from the tension caused by the incubus of doubt and uncertainty which so long controlled it, has stepped confidently forward to accept the situation confronting it oweing to the changed conditions." "Unfavorable circumstances . . . have hardly excited remark, while the stimulating effects have been so numerous and important as to surprise all but the most optimistic," this journal concluded. A new type of American empire, temporarily clothed in armor, stepped out on the international stage after a half century of preparation to make its claim as one of the great world powers.

9   *William McKinley*

        The President Asks for War

In February of 1898 two events exacerbated friction between the United States and Spain. First came the theft and publication by W. R. Hearst of Enrique De Lôme's (the Spanish Minister at Washington) indiscreet letter denigrating McKinley as "weak and a bidder for the admiration of the crowd, besides being a would-be politician (politicastro) who tries to leave a door open behind himself while keeping on good terms with the jingoes of his party." Then, on 15 February, the second class battleship Maine was destroyed in Havana harbor by explosions of undetermined origin, with a death toll of 258 enlisted men and two officers. After resisting foreign pressures (including the Vatican) for mediation, McKinley asked Congress for a declaration of war on 11 April. Congress responded affirmatively eight days later (the actual date was 20 April at 2:45 a.m.), though not before attaching a self-denying ordinance (the Teller Amendment) with respect to the postwar acquisition of Cuba. In this message, note McKinley's conscious determination to link his policy to that of his presidential predecessor, and his continued refusal to grant belligerent status to the Cuban rebels, despite the imminence of war with Spain. Does his rationalization of the need for war throw any light on the positions of Pratt and LeFeber?

Obedient to that precept of the Constitution which commands the President to give from time to time to the Congress information of the state of the Union and to recommend to their con-

SOURCE. William McKinley, in *Papers Relating to the Foreign Relations of the United States, 1898,* Washington: Government Printing Office, 1901, pp. 750–760.

sideration such measures as he shall judge necessary and expedient, it becomes my duty now to address your body with regard
to the grave crisis that has arisen in the relations of the United
States to Spain by reason of the warfare that for more than three
years has raged in the neighboring island of Cuba.

I do so because of the intimate connection of the Cuban question with the state of our own Union and the grave relation the
course which it is now incumbent upon the nation to adopt must
needs bear to the traditional policy of our Government if it is
to accord with the precepts laid down by the founders of the
Republic and religiously observed by succeeding Administrations
to the present day. . . .

Since the present revolution began, in February, 1895, this
country has seen the fertile domain at our threshold ravaged by
fire and sword in the course of a struggle unequaled in the history
of the island and rarely paralleled as to the numbers of the
combatants and the bitterness of the contest by any revolution
of modern times where a dependent people striving to be free
have been opposed by the power of the sovereign state.

Our people have beheld a once prosperous community reduced
to comparative want, its lucrative commerce virtually paralyzed,
its exceptional productiveness diminished, its fields laid waste,
its mills in ruins, and its people perishing by tens of thousands
from hunger and destitution. We have found ourselves constrained, in the observance of that strict neutrality which our
laws enjoin, and which the law of nations commands, to police
our own waters and watch our own seaports in prevention of
any unlawful act in aid of the Cubans.

Our trade has suffered; the capital invested by our citizens in
Cuba has been largely lost, and the temper and forbearance of
our people have been so sorely tried as to beget a perilous unrest
among our own citizens which has inevitably found its expression
from time to time in the National Legislature, so that issues
wholly external to our own body politic engross attention and
stand in the way of that close devotion to domestic advancement
that becomes a self-contained commonwealth whose primal
maxim has been the avoidance of all foreign entanglements.
All this must needs awaken, and has, indeed, aroused the utmost

concern on the part of this Government, as well during my predecessor's term as in my own.

In April, 1896, the evils from which our country suffered through the Cuban war became so onerous that my predecessor made an effort to bring about a peace through the mediation of this Government in any way that might tend to an honorable adjustment of the contest between Spain and her revolted colony, on the basis of some effective scheme of self-government for Cuba under the flag and sovereignty of Spain. It failed through the refusal of the Spanish Government then in power to consider any form of mediation or, indeed, any plan of settlement which did not begin with the actual submission of the insurgents to the mother country, and then only on such terms as Spain herself might see fit to grant. The war continued unabated. The resistance of the insurgents was in no wise diminished. . . .

By the time the present administration took office a year ago, reconcentration—so called—had been made effective over the better part of the four central and western provinces, Santa Clara, Mantanzas, Habana, and Pinar del Rio.

The agricultural population to the estimated number of 300,000 or more was herded within the towns and their immediate vicinage, deprived of the means of support, rendered destitute of shelter, left poorly clad, and exposed to the most unsanitary conditions. As the scarcity of food increased with the devastation of the depopulated areas of production, destitution and want became misery and starvation. Month by month the death rate increased in an alarming ratio. By March, 1897, according to conservative estimates from official Spanish sources, the mortality among the reconcentrados from starvation and the diseases thereto incident exceeded 50 per centum of their total number.

No practical relief was accorded to the destitute. The overburdened towns, already suffering from the general dearth, could give no aid. So called "zones of cultivation" established within the immediate areas of effective military control about the cities and fortified camps proved illusory as a remedy for the suffering. The unfortunates, being for the most part women and children, with aged and helpless men, enfeebled by disease and hunger, could not have tilled the soil without tools, seed, or shelter for their own support or for the supply of the cities. Reconcentration, adopted avowedly as a war measure in order to cut off the resources of the insurgents, worked its predestined result. As I said in my message of last December, it was not civilized warfare; it was extermination. The only peace it could beget was that of the wilderness and the grave.

Meanwhile the military situation in the island had undergone a noticeable change. The extraordinary activity that characterized the second year of the war, when the insurgents invaded even the thitherto unharmed fields of Pinar del Rio and carried havoc and destruction up to the walls of the city of Havana itself, had relapsed into a dogged struggle in the central and eastern provinces. The Spanish arms regained a measure of control in Pinar del Rio and parts of Havana, but, under the existing conditions of the rural country, without immediate improvement of their productive situation. Even thus partially restricted, the revolutionists held their own, and their conquest and submission, put forward by Spain as the essential and sole basis of peace, seemed as far distant as at the outset.

In this state of affairs my Administration found itself confronted with the grave problem of its duty. My message of last December reviewed the situation and narrated the steps taken with a view to relieving its acuteness and opening the way to some form of honorable settlement. The assassination of the prime minister, Canovas, led to a change of government in Spain. The former administration, pledged to subjugation without concession, gave place to that of a more liberal party, committed long in advance to a policy of reform, involving the wider principle of home rule for Cuba and Puerto Rico.

The overtures of this Government, made through its new envoy, General Woodford, and looking to an immediate and effective amelioration of the condition of the island, although not accepted to the extent of admitted mediation in any shape, were met by assurances that home rule, in advanced phase, would be forthwith offered to Cuba, without waiting for the war to end, and that more humane methods should thenceforth prevail in the conduct of hostilities. Coincidentally with these declarations, the new Government of Spain continued and completed the policy already begun by its predecessor, of testifying friendly regard for this nation by releasing American citizens held under one charge or another connected with the insurrection, so that by the end of November not a single person entitled in any way to our national protection remained in a Spanish prison. . . .

The war in Cuba is of such a nature that short of subjugation or extermination a final military victory for either side seems impracticable. The alternative lies in the physical exhaustion of the one or the other party, or perhaps of both—a condition which in effect ended the ten years' war by the truce of Zanjon. The prospect of such a protraction and conclusion of the present strife is a contingency hardly to be contemplated with equanimity by the civilized world, and least of all by the United States, affected and injured as we are, deeply and intimately, by its very existence.

Realizing this, it appeared to be my duty, in a spirit of true friendliness, no less to Spain than to the Cubans who have so much to lose by the prolongation of the struggle, to seek to bring about an immediate termination of the war. To this end I submitted, on the 27th ultimo, as a result of much representation and correspondence, through the United States minister at Madrid, propositions to the Spanish Government looking to an armistice until October 1 for the negotiation of peace with the good offices of the President.

In addition, I asked the immediate revocation of the order of reconcentration, so as to permit the people to return to their farms and the needy to be relieved with provisions and supplies from the United States, cooperating with the Spanish authorities, so as to afford full relief.

The reply of the Spanish cabinet was received on the night of the 31st ultimo. It offered, as the means to bring about peace in Cuba, to confide the preparation thereof to the insular parliament, inasmuch as the concurrence of that body would be necessary to reach a final result, it being, however, understood that the powers reserved by the constitution to the central Government are not lessened or diminished. As the Cuban parliament does not meet until the 4th of May next, the Spanish Government would not object, for its part, to accept at once a suspension of hostilities if asked for by the insurgents from the general in chief, to whom it would pertain, in such case, to determine the duration and conditions of the armistice. . . .

I said in my message of December last, "It is to be seriously considered whether the Cuban insurrection possesses beyond dispute the attributes of statehood which alone can demand the recognition of belligerency in its favor." The same requirement must certainly be no less seriously considered when the graver issue of recognizing independence is in question, for no less positive test can be applied to the greater act than to the lesser; while, on the other hand, the influences and consequences of the struggle upon the internal policy of the recognizing State, which form important factors when the recognition of belligerency is concerned, are secondary, if not rightly eliminable, factors when the real question is whether the community claiming recognition is or is not independent beyond peradventure.

Nor from the standpoint of expediency do I think it would be wise or prudent for this Government to recognize at the present time the independence of the so-called Cuban Republic. Such recognition is not necessary in order to enable the United States to intervene and pacify the island. To commit this country now to the recognition of any particular government in Cuba might subject us to embarrassing conditions of international obligation toward the organization so recognized. In case of intervention our conduct would be subject to the approval or disapproval of such government. We would be required to submit to its direction and to assume to it the mere relation of a friendly ally.

When it shall appear hereafter that there is within the island a government capable of performing the duties and discharging the functions of a separate nation, and having, as a matter of fact, the proper forms and attributes of nationality, such government can be promptly and readily recognized and the relations and interests of the United States with such nation adjusted.

There remain the alternative forms of intervention to end the war, either as an impartial neutral by imposing a rational compromise between the contestants, or as the active ally of the one party or the other.

As to the first it is not to be forgotten that during the last few months the relation of the United States has virtually been one of friendly intervention in many ways, each not of itself conclusive, but all tending to the exertion of a potential influence toward an ultimate pacific result, just and honorable to all interests concerned. The spirit of all our acts hitherto has been an earnest, unselfish desire for peace and prosperity in Cuba, untarnished by differences between us and Spain, and unstained by the blood of American citizens.

The forcible intervention of the United States as a neutral to stop the war, according to the large dictates of humanity and following many historical precedents where neighboring States have interfered to check the hopeless sacrifices of life by internecine conflicts beyond their borders, is justifiable on rational grounds. It involves, however, hostile constraint upon both the parties to the contest as well to enforce a truce as to guide the eventual sattlement.

The grounds for such intervention may be briefly summarized as follows:

First. In the cause of humanity and to put an end to the barbarities, bloodshed, starvation, and horrible miseries now existing there, and which the parties to the conflict are either unable or unwilling to stop or mitigate. It is no answer to say this is all in another country, belonging to another nation, and is therefore none of our business. It is specially our duty, for it is right at our door.

Second. We owe it to our citizens in Cuba to afford them that protection and indemnity for life and property which no government there can or will afford, and to that end to terminate the conditions that deprive them of legal protection.

Third. The right to intervene may be justified by the very serious injury to the commerce, trade, and business of our people, and by the wanton destruction of property and devastation of the island.

Fourth, and which is of the utmost importance. The present condition of affairs in Cuba is a constant menace to our peace, and entails upon this Government an enormous expense. With such a conflict waged for years in an island so near us and with which our people have such trade and business relations; when the lives and liberty of our citizens are in constant danger and their property destroyed and themselves ruined; where our trading vessels are liable to seizure and are seized at our very door by war ships of a foreign nation, the expeditions of filibustering that we are powerless to prevent altogether, and the irritating questions and entanglements thus arising—all these and others that I need not mention, with the resulting strained relations, are a constant menace to our peace, and compel us to keep on a semiwar footing with a nation with which we are at peace.

These elements of danger and disorder already pointed out have been strikingly illustrated by a tragic event which has deeply and justly moved the American people. I have already transmitted to Congress the report of the naval court of inquiry on the destruction of the battle ship *Maine* in the harbor of Havana during the night of the 15th of February. The destruction of that noble vessel has filled the national heart with inexpressible horror. Two hundred and fifty-eight brave sailors and marines and two officers of our Navy, reposing in the fancied security of a friendly harbor, have been hurled to death, grief and want brought to their homes, and sorrow to the nation.

The naval court of inquiry, which, it is needless to say, commands the unqualified confidence of the Government, was unanimous in its conclusion that the destruction of the *Maine* was caused by an exterior explosion, that of a submarine mine. It did not assume to place the responsibility. That remains to be fixed.

In any event the destruction of the *Maine*, by whatever exterior cause, is a patent and impressive proof of a state of things in Cuba that is intolerable. That condition is thus shown to be such that the Spanish Government can not assure safety and security to a vessel of the American Navy in the harbor of Havana on a mission of peace, and rightfully there.

Further referring in this connection to recent diplomatic correspondence, a dispatch from our minister to Spain, of the 26th ultimo, contained the statement that the Spanish minister for foreign affairs assured him positively that Spain will do all that the highest honor and justice require in the matter of the *Maine*. The reply above referred to of the 31st ultimo also contained an expression of the readiness of Spain to submit to an arbitration all the differences which can arise in this matter, which is subsequently explained by the note of the Spanish minister at Washington of the 10th instant, as follows:

"As to the question of fact which springs from the diversity of views between the reports of the American and Spanish boards, Spain proposes that the facts be ascertained by an impartial investigation by experts, whose decision Spain accepts in advance."

To this I have made no reply. . . .

The long trial has proved that the object for which Spain has waged the war can not be attained. The fire of insurrection may flame or may smolder with varying seasons, but it has not been and it is plain that it can not be extinguished by present methods. The only hope of relief and repose from a condition which can no longer be endured is the enforced pacification of Cuba. In the name of humanity, in the name of civilization, in behalf of endangered American interests which give us the right and the duty to speak and to act, the war in Cuba must stop.

In view of these facts and of these considerations, I ask the Congress to authorize and empower the President to take measures to secure a full and final termination of hostilities between the Government of Spain and the people of Cuba, and to secure in the island the establishment of a stable government, capable of maintaining order and observing its international obligations, insuring peace and tranquility and the security of its citizens as well as our own, and to use the military and naval forces of the United States as may be necessary for these purposes.

And in the interest of humanity and to aid in preserving the lives of the starving people of the island I recommend that the distribution of food and supplies be continued, and that an appropriation be made out of the public Treasury to supplement the charity of our citizens.

The issue is now with the Congress. It is a solemn responsibility I have exhausted every effort to relieve the intolerable condition of affairs which is at our doors. Prepared to execute every obligation imposed upon me by the Constitution and the law, I await your action.

Yesterday, and since the preparation of the foregoing message, official information was received by me that the latest decree of the Queen Regent of Spain directs General Blanco, in order to prepare and facilitate peace, to proclaim a suspension of hostilities, the duration and details of which have not yet been communicated to me.

This fact with every other pertinent consideration will, I am sure, have your just and careful attention in the solemn deliberations upon which you are about to enter. If this measure attains a successful result, then our aspirations as a Christian, peace-loving people will be realized. If it fails, it will be only another justification for our contemplated action.

WILLIAM McKINLEY

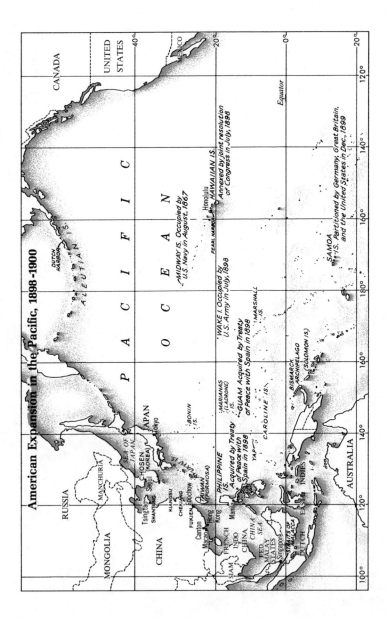

American Expansion in the Pacific, 1898-1900

CANADA

UNITED STATES

RUSSIA

MANCHURIA

MONGOLIA

CHINA

JAPAN

CHOSEN (KOREA)

TAIWAN (FORMOSA)

PHILIPPINE IS.
Acquired by Treaty
of Peace with
Spain in 1898

AUSTRALIA

DUTCH EAST INDIES

FRENCH INDO CHINA

SIAM

P A C I F I C   O C E A N

MIDWAY IS. Occupied by
U.S. Navy in August, 1867

HAWAIIAN IS.
Annexed by joint resolution
of Congress in July, 1898

Honolulu

PEARL HARBOR

WAKE I. Occupied by
U.S. Army in July, 1898

GUAM Acquired by Treaty
of Peace with Spain in 1898

MARIANAS
(LADRONE)
IS.

CAROLINE IS.

YAP

MARSHALL
IS.

BISMARCK
ARCHIPELAGO

SOLOMON IS.

SAMOA
IS. Partitioned by Germany, Great Britain,
and the United States in Dec., 1899

Equator

ALEUTIAN IS.

DUTCH HARBOR

SEA OF JAPAN

Tokyo

BONIN
IS.

Seoul

Tsingtao
SHANTUNG
KIANGSU
CHEKIANG
FUKIEN

Canton
Macao
Hong Kong
Amoy
Foochow

CHINA
SEA

JAVA SEA

FED.
MALAY
STATES
Singapore

STRAITS SET.

Manila

MEXICO

100°   120°   140°   160°   180°   160°   140°   120°

40°

20°

0°

20°

PART THREE

The Decision to Take Hawaii
and the Philippines

THE DECISION TO TAKE
HAWAII AND THE PHILIPPINES

10   *Thomas A. Bailey*

Without the War Hawaii Might Never Have Been Ours

Educated at Stanford (Ph.D., 1927), where he studied under the famous E. D. Adams, Thomas A. Bailey (1902–   ) taught at his alma mater from 1930 until his retirement in 1968. The author of several outstanding monographs on various aspects of modern U.S. diplomacy (especially during the period of World War I), Bailey's textbook on American diplomatic history has probably outsold all its competitors combined. This essay, one of his first forays into the area of diplomatic history, was originally published in 1931, and revised in form more than substance, for publication in a collected edition of his essays that appeared in 1969. He was one of the first American scholars to delve deeply into the territorial archives during his residence in Hawaii, and his principal arguments have held up well over the passage of the years. Note the emphasis that Bailey places on the interlocking relationships of thought and action among annexationists in the islands and on the mainland.

In 1893 the white property owners in Hawaii, chiefly American or American descended, forcibly overthrew the decadent Ha-

SOURCE. Thomas A. Bailey, "The United States and Hawaii During the Spanish-American War," in Alexander DeConde and Armin Rappaport, eds., *Essays Diplomatic and Undiplomatic of Thomas A. Bailey*, New York: Appleton-Century-Crofts, Educational Division, Meredith Corporation, 1969, pp. 89–103. Reprinted by permission of the publisher and the author.

waiian monarchy and established a republic. Their coup might have failed without the open support, both moral and military, of the United States minister in Honolulu, representing the Republican Administration of President Harrison. A treaty of annexation, hastily drafted in Washington with representatives of Hawaii, was rushed to the United States Senate. But the sands of the Harrison Administration ran out, and President Cleveland, a Democrat, took over. Suspecting foul play, he withdrew the pact from the Senate and subsequently revealed such strong opposition to the acquisition of the islands that the annexationists, both in Hawaii and in the United States, abandoned all hope of attaining their objective while he occupied the White House.

On June 16, 1897, the recently inaugurated President McKinley, a Republican, submitted a new treaty of annexation. Although supported by a majority of the senators, it was unable to command the necessary two-thirds vote. It was still languishing in the Senate nearly a year later, when war between Spain and the United States appeared imminent; and the Hawaiian authorities themselves conceded that approval was virtually impossible. In the event of Spanish-American hostilities, several courses lay open to the Honolulu government: first a proclamation of neutrality; second, silence and passivity; third, acquiescence in a wartime occupation of Hawaii by the Americans; and fourth, active assistance to the United States.

A large and influential group in Hawaii, composed chiefly of royalists and foreigners, feared property losses through Spanish reprisals or postwar claims. They therefore demanded an immediate proclamation of neutrality, even going so far as to urge foreign residents to appeal to their respective governments for protection. The French commissioner in Honolulu announced his intention of joining the representatives of the other powers in action that would insure adequate protection of foreigners in Hawaii. This, of course, would be a kind of interference that the United States could not have viewed with equanimity.

But the Hawaiian government had no assurance that Spain would respect a declaration of neutrality. Madrid could argue with considerable force that since Hawaii had officially consented to a treaty surrendering her sovereignty to the United States, she was, in spirit if not in fact, a part of the United States. The Hawaiian officials agreed, moreover, that a positive stand for neutrality would be interpreted by Americans as nothing short of a slap in the face. It might ruin whatever chances remained of annexation, the specific end for which the existing Honolulu regime had been formed.

For a time a policy of silence and passivity on the part of Hawaii received some, although not very serious, consideration. Such a course, although somewhat objectionable, was preferable to avowed neutrality. But with the outbreak of hostilities active measures were considered more desirable. The Hawaiian representatives in Washington were especially concerned about protecting their tiny republic until such time as annexation could be consummated, while securing for the United States the strategic advantages of the islands. They therefore drafted a bill authorizing McKinley to use Hawaii for war purposes, and sent it on to Honolulu for approval. But the scheme met with such serious opposition, both in the Hawaiian cabinet and in the legislature, that it was not even submitted to the latter body for approval. Among the objections were doubts as to the precise meaning of this proposed measure, an inability to discover whether it had the approval of Washington, differences of opinion as to its constitutionality from the standpoint of both America and Hawaii, and fear that such a step would permanently endanger annexation by permitting the United States in the future to assume control over the islands only when it was convenient and profitable to do so.

The joint resolution of annexation subsequently introduced into Congress appeared to be a far more satisfactory substitute, although in the event of its failure to pass, President McKinley might find authority to use Honolulu for war purposes under the provisions of existing treaties. McKinley may in fact have entertained the idea of resorting to occupation by executive action as a last expedient. When the Senate minority was opposing the passage of the joint resolution, Henry Cabot Lodge wrote: "...I do not believe the Senate can hold out very long, for the President has been very firm about it and means to annex

the Islands any way. I consider the Hawaiian business as practically settled."

The fourth possible course—and the one eventually adopted
by the Hawaiian government—was the rendering of active assistance prior to and without any definite assurance of annexation.
As a matter of fact, the Honolulu regime at no time favored
neutrality, and from the beginning of hostilities was eager to do
everything within its power to aid the United States. Nevertheless, there were several problems that had seriously to be considered before an actual proffer of assistance could be made.
The oldest proannexation newspaper in the islands, although
favoring an abandonment of neutrality, wondered how far "we
the annexationists and the dominant power here, numbering a
small percentage of the inhabitants, have the right to push men,
women, and children, who largely outnumber us and do not
agree with us, into the risks of war. . . ."

The Honolulu government itself was chiefly puzzled to know
whether outspoken adherence to the fortunes of the United States
would embarrass that nation by increasing its war responsibilities.
Not desiring to take any steps without ascertaining American
wishes, President Dole addressed two dispatches to the Hawaiian
minister in Washington, F. M. Hatch, instructing him to sound
out McKinley. But before a reply was received, news of the
outbreak of war reached Hawaii on May 7, 1898. On the following day, Dole, as a result of several conferences with his cabinet,
sent a telegram requesting Hatch to ascertain what McKinley
wanted the Hawaiian government to do. In case McKinley
appeared to favor such a course, Hatch was to "tender to the
President the support of this Government in the pending
conflict," even to the extent of negotiating a treaty of alliance.

President McKinley greatly appreciated the attitude of the
Hawaiian government and promised to make known the wishes
of the United States as circumstances developed. But he did
not care to go into details about the formal offer just at that
time because he believed that Congress would speedily annex
the islands. This proffer of assistance before the news of Dewey's
victory had come to Hawaii, and in the face of strong local opposition, aroused much more sympathy for the Hawaiian cause in

the United States than would otherwise have been possible. It undoubtedly had much to do with the passing of the joint resolution of annexation.

Several weeks before the outbreak of hostilities, L. A. Thurston, a Hawaiian treaty commissioner in Washington who hoped to score a point for annexation, suggested to the Navy Department the desirability of buying all of the available coal in Honolulu for war purposes. Immediately Theodore Roosevelt, then Assistant Secretary of the Navy, began to dictate letters and send off dispatches for that purpose. The purchases were made, and on April 12, 1898, the Hawaiian executive council, on application from the United States consul general, voted to allow four additional esplanade lots for storage purposes. Dole considered this action, if not an actual breach of neutrality, a definite commitment to the side of the United States.

With the outbreak of hostilities, the republic of Hawaii, realizing that it would have to pay the price if a Spanish cruiser should appear, extended every possible kind of help to the United States. The islands in fact became a base for operations against the Philippines. A movement to put a battalion of Hawaiian volunteers in Cuba was abandoned only when word came from Washington explaining that more troops could not be used. During the course of the conflict three Philippine-bound transport fleets called at Honolulu, and on every occasion from 3,000 to 5,000 American soldiers were fed and entertained for several days. The civilian population did its utmost to cultivate annexation sentiment among the troops by a lavish display of sympathy and hospitality. The Hawaiian officials, hoping that the soldiers would indirectly impress upon Congress the desirability of possessing the islands, actually turned them loose with an abundance of writing material in the house and senate chambers. The Spanish government was naturally aware of these violations of neutrality, but in the circumstances the forthcoming protest from its vice consul at Honolulu received scant attention.

The position of Dewey after his victory at Manila gave an unexpected twist to the Hawaii question. As the annexation treaty before the Senate appeared to have no reasonable hope of success, the Administration proposed a joint resolution. It was promptly introduced into the House on May 4, 1898, and reported out by the Committee on Foreign Affairs on May 17, 1898. Significantly, another joint resolution, supplemented by an elaborate report, had been presented by the Senate Committee on Foreign Relations on March 16, 1898, but no further action had resulted. The failure of this joint resolution, and the introduction of the successful one almost immediately after the news of Dewey's victory, revealed a new appreciation of the strategic importance of Hawaii.

Throughout the ensuing debates in Congress, dozens of reasons were presented for and against the acquisition of Hawaii. But most of them had already been discussed at great length during the preceding five years. The position of the islands in relation to the war enabled the annexationists to emphasize three strong arguments, two of which were new and a third of which, although previously considered, appeared in a far stronger light. First, the attitude of the United States toward Hawaii was morally unsound; second, Hawaii was indispensable for the successful prosecution of the war; and third, Hawaii was necessary for the defense of the Pacific seaboard and the Philippines.

The moral argument had considerable force. The United States was flagrantly violating the neutrality of the islands, even though Washington had given formal notice of the existence of war to the other powers (so that they might proclaim neutrality), and was jealously watching their behavior. The position of America was all the more reprehensible in that she was compelling a weak people to violate the international law that she had in large measure strengthened by her own stand on the *Alabama* claims of Civil War memory. Furthermore, in line with the precedent established by the Geneva arbitral award of 1872, Hawaii would be liable for every cent of damage caused by her dereliction as a neutral, and for the Americans to force her into this position was cowardly and ungrateful. At the end of the war, Spain or cooperating powers might occupy Hawaii indefinitely, if not permanently, to insure payment of damages, with a consequent jeopardizing of the defenses of the Pacific Coast.

The reply of the anti-annexationists was that Hawaii, in return for past protection of independence and favorable tariff arrangements, owed many times over whatever favors she was conferring on the United States. Washington, moreover, was in a position to assume any claims for damages against Hawaii, or to compel prostrate Spain to free Hawaii from liability. To be sure, the payment of money by the United States would not right a wrong; but, on the other hand, Spain would experience difficulty in establishing a case. Although the islands were admittedly flouting neutrality, they had nothing to do with Dewey's victory, and it could not be demonstrated that they were responsible for the loss of the Philippines. One may conclude, therefore that although the moral argument was undeniably a powerful one, its appeal was more emotional than practical.

The argument that annexation was imperative for prosecuting the war in the Philippines carried, whatever its merits, great weight both in Congress and out. Dewey, surrounded by millions of Spanish subjects, was in grave need of reinforcements, and not to send them to him as speedily as possible would be an act of the basest ingratitude. A coaling station in the Pacific was necessary, for there were only two ships in the Navy that could steam from San Francisco to Manila without recoaling. Colliers might be used, but they were slow, uneconomical, and dangerously uncertain in rough weather. Although the United States had long-term rights to a coaling station at Pearl Harbor, there was no coal there and the inlet could not then be entered by warships. Furthermore, the islands were believed necessary for the health of the soldiers confined on the transports.

The anti-annexationists, on the other hand, pointed out that it would be possible to save more than 400 miles over the Hawaiian route by sailing from San Francisco to the Philippines by way of the Aleutian Islands. There the United States already had Kiska, a far more commodious harbor than that of Honolulu. Although there was no coaling station at Kiska, the Navy could rather easily send ahead a fleet of colliers and establish one. Furthermore, there were a number of ships in the service that could not sail all the way from Honolulu to Manila without exhausting their coal supply, but there was not a single ship that would have to recoal at sea if it went from San Francisco to Manila by way of Kiska. In addition, the chilly northern route would be more healthful for the troops.

The annexationists objected that the Kiska route was undesirable because of ice, shoals, fog, currents, and storms, whereas in Hawaii these drawbacks were absent. Besides, there were shops in Honolulu capable of handling almost any repairs. But the difficulties of the northerly voyage were evidently exaggerated. Anti-annexationists pointed out that the Canadian Pacific line, which had made the quickest recorded trips for the crossing of the Pacific, used the route a little south of the Aleutians summer and winter. Moreover, vessels leaving San Francisco for Japan did not waste the additional time necessary for touching at Honolulu unless they had special business there.

In evaluating the war-measure argument one should note that, assuming the usefulness of the islands for war purposes, there was no need to annex them. Without possession, the Americans were reaping every possible benefit they could have received had the islands been a part of their territory. And these favors, bestowed largely for the purpose of cultivating annexation sentiment, would probably not have been forthcoming so generously if the islands had been annexed.

One may also question the need for excessive haste in reinforcing Dewey. There was no Spanish fleet left in Asiatic waters, and Dewey had Manila at the mercy of his guns. The departure of Camara's fleet from Cadiz on June 16, 1898, had no appreciable bearing on annexation, for that event was not even mentioned in the debates. Nor was the possibility of trouble from the German fleet at Manila more than suggested, and by the time the joint resolution passed the Senate, Dewey had received sufficient reinforcements to strengthen himself against a possible German attack. But even if these two threats had appeared to Congress to be serious, help could not have been rushed to Dewey sooner if Hawaii had been a part of the United States.

Nor could annexationists demonstrate that Hawaii was indispensable for the relief of Dewey. Colliers could have been employed, and a coaling station, although it had drawbacks, could have been established, as noted, on the shorter Kiska route.

*Morgan provide conclusive evidence in determining the sources of
McKinley's inspiration for the decision to expand overseas?*

McKinley, though hardly ignorant of either the battle [of
Manila] or its consequences, was as ill-equipped as many sub-
ordinates, and at first followed the action of a schoolbook map of
the Orient. A member of the Coast and Geodetic Survey took him
a detailed chart of the Philippines. After a half hour's talk, he
bowed out his visitors with a remark applicable to many of his
countrymen: "It is evident that I must learn a great deal of
geography in this war...."

The very name "Philippines" drew a blank with most Americans, and Mr. Dooley later said he thought they were canned
goods. But it did not really matter; the Stars and Stripes flew
somewhere. On May 2, before Dewey's victory was confirmed,
McKinley in conference with military and diplomatic advisors
authorized a relief expedition to the islands. General Wesley
Merritt was ordered to assault Manila with a force of regulars
and volunteers, whose first contingent would shortly leave from
San Francisco.

The battle was no sooner reported than Americans rushed to
their maps. Then in a second breath many demanded retention
of the islands as spoils of war and outposts of Oriental empire.
Though cautious administration spokesmen held their tongues,
the expansionist press began its long rallying cry. "Common
sense tells us to keep what has cost so much to wrest from an
unworthy foe," said a Baltimore paper. "Back of that is the
solid, irresistible sentiment of the people."

Suspicions of foreign powers and their designs in the Orient
intensified this emerging demand for empire. Germany, France,
Great Britain, Japan, and heaven knew who else had ships and
agents in the Orient; if America did not take the Philippines,
they would, many reasoned. This would be disastrous for
American diplomacy and trade in the East. As usual, congressmen
were more outspoken than men in the administration. "The
fear I have about this war is that peace will be declared before

we can get full occupation of the Philippines and Porto Rico," Senator Frye said bluntly. . . .

Opinion over retaining the islands was divided within the administration. As July closed and the President had said nothing beyond the usual generalities, those around him felt he was "conservative" on the issue. To one visitor, however, he showed clearly that he already favored overseas expansion. He wanted to retain as little as possible from the war's conquests, but he did not yet know how much that little would be. He thought that "the general principle of holding on to what we get" was wise. If events dictated, he would keep all the archipelago. Impressed by the President's words and his whole demeanor, his listener promptly assured Senator Lodge that McKinley was an expansionist. From the very first, McKinley inclined toward retaining all the Philippines. He now deftly and circuitously began to develop public opinion to support his decision.

McKinley showed his sympathies with expansion by using the war emergency to annex Hawaii. He had always considered this a consummation of long-standing Republican policy, not an innovation. He permitted the annexation treaty to languish until the war because he was unwilling to add it to his burdens in dealing with Cuba. Members of his own party opposed Hawaiian annexation. In the House, Speaker Reed showed members with a piece of string and a terrestial globe that the distance from the United States to Asia was shorter via the already American-owned Aleutian Islands than through Hawaii. He convinced few, and missed the essential point; annexation was never of the head but of the heart. In July, using the war and its resulting need for naval bases in the Pacific, pointing out that Hawaii would be the major stepping stone to American penetration in the Orient, the administration pushed through a joint resolution annexing the islands, and the President signed it on July 7. By now resistance to the scheme was futile. Senator Hoar favored it, saying in justification for his divided stand on expansion that the Hawaiians welcomed American rule, while the Filipinos did not. The expansionists easily saw Hawaii's importance; it was a beginning, not an end. If it could be acquired, what would stop acquisition of the Philippines? "To maintain our flag in the Philippines, we must raise our flag in Hawaii," the New York *Sun* said candidly.

The situation in the Philippines was much more complicated. The Filipinos welcomed Americans there as liberators, not as conquerors. Like the Cubans, they had long been in revolt against the Spanish, and claimed a George Washington in the person of Emilio Aguinaldo. Always jealous of his prerogatives, and claiming to head a genuinely popular Philippine Republic, Aguinaldo watched Dewey and his ships with suspicion. For the moment their guns only dominated the Spanish forts; but who could tell what the Americans would do after a land force arrived and they invaded the islands? The Filipinos and Americans were nervous allies.

Alive to the dangers involved, the State Department quickly forbade any diplomatic communication with or promise to the insurgents. Washington insisted that the islands were under American control alone until a peace treaty settled their fate. Though he worried over the "insurgent complication," as he called it, the politically inept Dewey never really understood the problem. His wavering advice to officials at home further complicated an already touchy problem. In June Aguinaldo ominously proclaimed his republic, with himself as President.

To counter this tension and to relieve Dewey, the first Army contingent left San Francisco on May 25. Its commander brought the President's instructions. McKinley said nothing of Philippine independence, but promised cooperation and kindness; events would formulate a firmer policy as soon as he had adequate information. He held out a slender, unspoken hope of self-rule. In the meantime, "Our occupation should be as free from severity as possible."

. . . in early August McKinley's mind turned to making peace. Indirectly the Spanish had already begun to ask for armistice terms. On July 18 Spain asked the French to state her case. Due to official delay, negotiations did not begin until July 22, when the French Ambassador, Jules Cambon, hurriedly asked McKinley to outline his armistice terms. Cambon had no sooner left than McKinley summoned his cabinet and advisors to discuss the crucial problem in any armistice: what to do with the Philippines. The President did not force his views, but listened patiently to all, discovering that his cabinet remained divided. Some members wanted all the islands, some wanted none of the islands, and others seemed ready to take a naval station at Manila and leave the rest of the archipelago to Spain. Since General Merritt's army had not yet taken the city, it seemed impossible to claim the islands by right of conquest.

The President now exercised his charm and disingenuous tact. He invited the cabinet for a ride on the Potomac to escape Washington's heat. On a hot day the stiffly attired statesmen embarked on a lighthouse tender for a river cruise where there were no prying eyes or ears. The President heard everyone patiently. Day wanted only a naval base; Treasury Secretary Lyman Gage agreed, but Interior Secretary Cornelius Bliss and Attorney-General Griggs saw commercial possibilities in taking all the islands. Secretary of Agriculture James Wilson, an old friend and valued political ally of the President's, wanted to evangelize the islands. McKinley laughed, and his eyes twinkled: "Yes, you Scotch favor keeping everything, including the Sabbath."

Cabinet sessions followed on land as the men hammered opposing views into a single policy. Day's first draft of a statement would have retained only Luzon; McKinley buried it. By July 30 personal feelings in the cabinet were giving way; expansion won by a narrow majority when the men voted. After one session Day had remarked: "Mr. President, you didn't put my motion for a naval base." McKinley, who had already remarked that Day only wanted a "hitching post" in the Philippines, replied sagely: "No, Judge, I was afraid it would carry!"

Expansion won in the final tally, though the President deftly left the question of retaining the Philippines open for settlement at the peace conference. Cambon sent Spain the President's outline and tried to soften the blow. The Americans demanded four points: (1) Spain would free Cuba entirely; (2) the United States would retain Puerto Rico as a war indemnity; (3) the armistice was a suspension, not an end, of hostilities; (4) the Americans would hold the city, bay, and harbor of Manila pending final disposition of the islands at the subsequent peace conference. When the Spanish protested that the United States could not claim the islands on the grounds of conquest, McKinley assured them soothingly that it would be best to leave the matter to the peace conferees. His mind was not made up either way, he said calmly. "The Madrid government may be assured that up to this time there is nothing determined *a priori* in my mind against Spain; likewise, I consider there is nothing decided against the United States." Further Spanish delay was futile, for McKinley would not soften American demands, and Cambon advised Madrid to face reality. The fighting stopped on August 12. . . .

McKinley had momentarily met the problem of overseas expansion in a characteristic manner; he left it to be solved at a later conference. He later revealed that this was his purpose all along. He had followed the cabinet's discussions largely to maneuver for support and hear opinion. When the final decision retained Manila and left the rest of the problem to negotiation, the President showed his private secretary a scrap of paper in his pocket on which he had written that exact solution days before. "If the American forces have remained until now in their positions it is in obedience to a duty with respect to residents and strangers and the progress of affairs imposes upon them," he told the Spanish. It was a roundabout way of saying that the Americans would remain in Manila more or less permanently.

In leaving the Philippine question open to later settlement, McKinley committed his administration to retaining them. Whatever he might infer to the contrary in his few and guarded public utterances, he knew that postponement would develop and focus public opinion in support of his decision to retain the islands. His whole tone as well as his actions indicated that he had made up his own mind. He had annexed Hawaii with allusions to manifest destiny; he had ordered Dewey to the Philippines, knowing what consequences might follow; he had dispatched a land force to conquer those islands; and he had conducted himself during peace negotiations as only an expansionist could. There was only one time at which he could have spurned the Philippines and committed his administration against overseas expansion, and that was the day after Dewey's victory. To delay either way after that merely invited public opinion to "demand" retention. Now that peace had come, he would bide his time, delay proceedings while he sounded the public temper, and subtly maneuver blocs of support into his columns. In the end he adroitly appeared to "capitulate" and accept the islands, just as he had "capitulated" to demand to free Cuba.

Though relieved by peace, the President knew that his troubles would continue. His own changed status merely symbolized his country's new course. She had defeated a supposedly major European power, thrust herself upon the attention of every government in the world, showed her latent military power, and acquired an empire. It seemed to come suddenly, but the wise man knew that 1898 merely symbolized the end of a very long, complicated, and logical emergence to world power. Old issues were dying, like youth and middle years, a man could enter public life speaking for one great issue, and retire after a long career with that issue still in the forefront of public affairs. The tariff, the currency, the South, internal improvements—all now seemed outmoded. War brought new responsibilities, new problems. He would be the first president to have no rest from complicated foreign issues, just as his generation of Americans would be the first to pursue more than "crisis diplomacy." Foreign affairs were here to stay. Responsibility would be the price of greatness.

*　*　*　*　*

12   *William McKinley*

Instructions to the Peace Commissioners

Having decided in advance of the peace negotiations to take the entire Philippine archipelago, McKinley chose a delegation that would carry out these desires, but would seemingly represent the various

SOURCE. William McKinley, "Instructions to the Peace Commissioners," dated 16 September 1898, in *Papers Relating to the Foreign Relations of the United States, 1898*, Washington: Government Printing Office, 1901, pp. 904–908.

*divisions in the country. Chosen to head the delegation was William R.
Day, a former law associate from McKinley's home town of Canton,
Ohio, then serving as Secretary of State. Somewhat predisposed against
the acquisition of overseas territories, Day could still be relied upon to
carry out McKinley's wishes.*

*Three of the delegates were outspoken expansionists: Whitelaw Reid,
editor of the New York Tribune; and Cushman K. Davis (R-Minn.) and
William P. Frye (R-Me.), both members of the Senate Foreign Relations
Committee. McKinley then sought out an anti-expansion Democrat,
Associate Justice Edward D. White, but, following a meeting between
the two in Cleveland, White was dropped from consideration. McKinley
then chose Senator George Gray (D-Del.), an anti-expansionist member
of the Foreign Relations Committee, offering him a federal judgeship
as a reward for serving, should he fail to gain re-election to the Senate.*

*The day before departure, the peace delegation (with the exception
of Gray who, because of the lateness of his appointment, was still making
travel arrangements) met with McKinley to receive their official instructions. Note the carefully worded sections pertaining to the Philippines,
especially the references to the "commercial opportunity" and the
"open door."*

Executive Mansion,
Washington, September 16, 1898.

By a protocol signed at Washington August 12, 1898, a copy
of which is herewith inclosed, it was agreed that the United
States and Spain would each appoint not more than five Commissioners to treat of peace, and that the Commissioners so appointed
should meet at Paris not later than October 1, 1898, and proceed
to the negotiation and conclusion of a treaty of peace, which
treaty should be subject to ratification according to the respective
constitutional forms of the two countries.

For the purpose of carrying into effect this stipulation, I have
appointed you as Commissioners on the part of the United
States to meet and confer with Commissioners on the part of
Spain.

As an essential preliminary to the agreement to appoint Commissioners to treat of peace, this Government required of that

of Spain the unqualified concession of the following precise demands:

(1) The relinquishment of all claim of sovereignty over and title to Cuba.

(2) The cession to the United States of Porto Rico and other islands under Spanish sovereignty in the West Indies.

(3) The cession of an island in the Ladrones, to be selected by the United States.

(4) The immediate evacuation by Spain of Cuba, Porto Rico, and other Spanish islands in the West Indies.

(5) The occupation by the United States of the city, bay, and harbor of Manila pending the conclusion of a treaty of peace which should determine the control, disposition, and government of the Philippines.

These demands were conceded by Spain, and their concession was, as you will perceive, solemnly recorded in the protocol of the 12th of August.

By article 1 of the instrument Spain agreed to "relinquish all claim of sovereignty over and title to Cuba."

By article 2 she agreed to "cede to the United States the island of Porto Rico and other islands now under Spanish sovereignty in the West Indies, and also an island in the Ladrones, to be selected by the United States."

By article 3 it was declared that the United States would "occupy and hold the city, bay, and harbor of Manila pending the conclusion of a treaty of peace which shall determine the control, disposition, and government of the Philippines."

By article 4 provision was made for the immediate evacuation of Cuba, Porto Rico, and other Spanish islands in the West Indies, as follows:

"Spain will immediately evacuate Cuba, Porto Rico, and other islands now under Spanish sovereignty in the West Indies; and to this end each Government will, within ten days after the signing of this protocol, appoint Commissioners, and the Commissioners so appointed shall, within thirty days after the signing of this protocol, meet at Habana for the purpose of arranging and carrying out the details of the aforesaid evacuation of Cuba and the adjacent Spanish islands; and each Government will, within ten days after the signing of this protocol, also appoint other Commissioners, who shall, within thirty days after the signing of this protocol, meet at San Juan, in Porto Rico, for the purpose of arranging and carrying out the details of the aforesaid evacuation of Porto Rico and other islands now under Spanish sovereignty in the West Indies."

The commissioners referred to in the foregoing article have been appointed, and they are now in session at Habana and San Juan, respectively. A copy of their instructions is herewith inclosed.

By these instructions you will observe that the evacuation of Cuba, Porto Rico, and other Spanish Islands in the West Indies is treated as a military operation, and will, when carried into effect, leave the evacuated places in the military occupation of the United States. The purposes of the United States during such occupation are set forth in General Order No. 101 of the War Department of July 18, 1898, which was issued by direction of the President on the capitulation of the Spanish forces at Santiago de Cuba and in the eastern part of the Province of Santiago and the occupation of the territory by the forces of the United States. A copy of this order is hereto annexed for your information.

As the evacuation of Cuba and the other Spanish islands in the West Indies by the Spanish military forces devolves upon the United States the duty of taking possession of and holding and preserving all the immovable property therein previously belonging to the Government of Spain, the evacuation commissioners of the United States are instructed to arrange for the taking into possession and to take into possession for the United States, all public buildings and grounds, forts, fortifications, arsenals, depots, docks, wharves, piers, and other fixed property previously belonging to Spain, and to arrange for the care and safe-keeping of such property under the authority and control of the United States. Small arms and accouterments, batteries of field artillery, supply and baggage wagons, ambulances, and other impedimenta of the Spanish army in Cuba and other Spanish islands in the West Indies are to be removed, if desired, by the representatives of Spain, provided such removal shall be effected within a reasonable time; but the armament of forts, fortifications, and fixed batteries, being in the nature of immovable fixtures, are not to be allowed to be taken, but are, in connection with such forts, fortifications, and batteries, to be taken over into the possession of the United States. The instructions of the evacuation commissioners also contain appropriate clauses in regard to the custody and preservation by the United States of state papers, public records, and other papers and documents necessary or convenient for the government of the islands, as well as all judicial and legal documents and other public records necessary or convenient for securing to individuals the titles to property.

It will be proper to confirm these transactions by appropriate clauses in the treaty of peace.

Similar clauses will be inserted in respect to the island ceded to the United States in the Ladrones. This Government has selected the Island of Guam, and you are instructed to embody in the treaty of peace a proper stipulation of cession.

A rumor has reached us from various quarters to the effect that the Spanish Peace Commissioners will be instructed to claim compensation for the public property of the Spanish Government in Cuba, as well as in territories agreed to be ceded to the United States. This rumor is not credited, but it is proper to make a few observations upon it. No such claim on the part of the Spanish Government is to be entertained in respect to any territory which Spain either cedes to the United States or as to which she relinquishes her sovereignty and title. The cession of territory or the relinquishment of sovereignty over and title to it is universally understood to carry with it the public property of the Government by which the cession or relinquishment is made. Any claim, therefore, on the part of Spain, such as that above suggested, would be inconsistent with the express agreements embodied in the protocol.

In the correspondence leading up to the signature of that

instrument you will observe that this Government waived, for the time being, the requirement of a pecuniary indemnity from Spain. This concession was made in the hope that Spain would thereby be enabled promptly to accept our terms. But if the Spanish Commissioners should, contrary to our just expectations, put forward and insist upon a claim for compensation for public property, you are instructed to put forward as a counterclaim a demand for an indemnity for the cost of the war.

By article 6 of the protocol it was agreed that hostilities between the two countries should be suspended, and that notice to that effect should be given as soon as possible by each Government to the commanders of its military and naval forces. Such notice was given by the Government of the United States immediately after the signature of the protocol, the forms of the necessary orders having previously been prepared. But before notice could reach the commanders of the military and naval forces of the United States in the Philippines they captured and took possession by conquest of the city of Manila and its suburbs, which are therefore held by the United States by conquest as well as by virtue of the protocol.

In view of what has taken place it is necessary now to determine what shall be our future relations to the Philippines. Before giving you specific instructions on this subject it is my desire to present certain general considerations.

It is my wish that throughout the negotiations intrusted to the Commission the purpose and spirit with which the United States accepted the unwelcome necessity of war should be kept constantly in view. We took up arms only in obedience to the dictates of humanity and in the fulfillment of highly public and moral obligations. We had no design of aggrandizement and no ambition of conquest. Through the long course of repeated representations which preceded and aimed to avert the struggle, and in the final arbitrament of force, this country was impelled solely by the purpose of relieving grievous wrongs and removing long-existing conditions which disturbed its tranquillity, which shocked the moral sense of mankind, and which could no longer be endured.

It is my earnest wish that the United States in making peace should follow the same high rule of conduct which guided it in facing war. It should be as scrupulous and magnanimous in the concluding settlement as it was just and humane in its original action. The luster and the moral strength attaching to a cause which can be confidently rested upon the considerate judgment of the world should not under any illusion of the hour be dimmed by ulterior designs which might tempt us into excessive demands or into an adventurous departure on untried paths. It is believed that the true glory and the enduring interests of the country will most surely be served if an unselfish duty conscientiously accepted and a signal triumph honorably achieved shall be crowned by such an example of moderation, restraint, and reason in victory as best comports with the traditions and character of our enlightened Republic.

Our aim in the adjustment of peace should be directed to lasting results and to the achievement of the common good under the demands of civilization, rather than to ambitious designs. The terms of the protocol were framed upon this consideration. The abandonment of the Western Hemisphere by Spain was an imperative necessity. In presenting that requirement, we only fulfilled a duty universally acknowledged. It involves no ungenerous reference to our recent foe, but simply a recognition of the plain teachings of history, to say that it was not compatible with the assurance of permanent peace on and near our own territory that the Spanish flag should remain on this side of the sea. This lesson of events and of reason left no alternative as to Cuba, Porto Rico, and the other islands belonging to Spain in this hemisphere.

The Philippines stand upon a different basis. It is none the less true, however, that, without any original thought of complete or even partial acquisition, the presence and success of our arms at Manila imposes upon us obligations which we can not disregard. The march of events rules and overrules human action. Avowing unreservedly the purpose which has animated all our effort, and still solicitous to adhere to it, we can not be unmindful that, without any desire or design on our part, the war has brought us new duties and responsibilities which we must meet and discharge as becomes a great nation on whose growth and career from the beginning the Ruler of Nations has plainly written the high command and pledge of civilization.

Incidental to our tenure in the Philippines is the commercial opportunity to which American statesmanship can not be indifferent. It is just to use every legitimate means for the enlargement of American trade; but we seek no advantages in the Orient which are not common to all. Asking only the open door for ourselves, we are ready to accord the open door to others. The commercial opportunity which is naturally and inevitably associated with this new opening depends less on large territorial possession than upon an adequate commercial basis and upon broad and equal privileges.

It is believed that in the practical application of these guiding principles the present interests of our country and the proper measure of its duty, its welfare in the future, and the consideration of its exemption from unknown perils will be found in full accord with the just, moral, and humane purpose which was invoked as our justification in accepting the war.

In view of what has been stated, the United States can not accept less than the cession in full right and sovereignty of the island of Luzon. It is desirable, however, that the United States shall acquire the right of entry for vessels and merchandise belonging to citizens of the United States into such ports of the Philippines as are not ceded to the United States upon terms of equal favor with Spanish ships and merchandise, both in relation to port and customs charges and rates of trade and commerce, together with other rights of protection and trade accorded to citizens of one country within the territory of another. You are therefore instructed to demand such concession, agreeing on your part that Spain shall have similar rights as to her subjects and vessels in the ports of any territory in the Philippines ceded to the United States.

We are informed that numerous persons are now held as prisoners by the Spanish Government for political acts performed in Cuba, Porto Rico, or other Spanish islands in the West Indies, as well as in the Philippines. You are instructed to demand the release of these prisoners, so far as their acts have connection with matters involved in the settlement between the United

States and Spain.

It will be desirable to insert in any treaty of peace which you may conclude a stipulation for the revival of the provisions of our former treaties with Spain, so far as they may be applicable to present conditions.

I have directed Gen. Wesley Merritt, the late commander at Manila, to report to the Commission at Paris, where he will arrive October 2, with such information as he may possess; and it is understood he will carry with him, for the use of the Commission, the views of Admiral Dewey. To the views of these distinguished officers I invite the most careful consideration of the Commission.

It is desired that your negotiations shall be conducted with all possible expedition, in order that the treaty of peace, if you should succeed in making one, may be submitted to the Senate early in the ensuing session. Should you at any time in the course of your negotiations desire further instructions, you will ask for them without delay.

WILLIAM McKINLEY

13   *Thomas J. McCormick*

The Philippines Were Insular Stepping Stones to the Chinese Pot of Gold

Thomas J. McCormick (1933–   ) is another historian who has been heavily influenced by the dynamic teaching and writings of Fred H. Harrington and William A. Williams under whom he studied at Wisconsin (Ph.D., 1960). Currently teaching at the University of Pittsburgh, he has also been swayed by the social science interdisciplinary technique

SOURCE. Thomas J. McCormick, "Insular Imperialism and the Open Door: The China Market and the Spanish-American War." Copyright 1963 by the Pacific Coast Branch, American Historical Association. Reprinted from *Pacific Historical Review*, Vol. XXXII, pp. 155–169, by permission of the Branch.

*approach to historical studies advocated by Samuel P. Hays and others.
As a result, many critics have categorized him as a rigid neo-Beardian
determinist. However, unlike some of his more illustrious critics,
McCormick applies himself to the central question of American imperialism during this period; viz., how did the McKinley Administration
develop the policy decisions that committed the nation to the annexation of the Philippines and the expanded commercial penetration of
China? Note the deft manner in which McCormick challenges some of
the standard assumptions of Pratt and Hofstadter, while adding to the
depth of Morgan's analysis of McKinley as a policy maker. Did the fear
of a potential partition of the Philippines by the European powers
(and Japan) precipitate the decision to demand the entire archipelago
from Spain? Would such a partition have inhibited American efforts
to gain entrée to the economic opportunities seemingly developing on
the Asian mainland?*

America's insular acquisitions of 1898 were not primarily products of "large policy" imperialism. Hawaii, Wake, Guam, and
the Philippines were not taken principally for their own economic
worth, or for their fulfillment of the Manifest Destiny credo, or
for their venting of the "psychic crisis." They were obtained, instead, largely in an eclectic effort to construct a system of coaling,
cable, and naval stations into an integrated trade route which
could facilitate realization of America's one overriding ambition
in the Pacific—the penetration and, ultimately, the domination
of the fabled China market. . . .

From the very beginning of the Spanish-American War, the
McKinley administration intended to retain a foothold in the
Philippines as an "American Hong Hong," a commercial *entrepôt* to the China market and a center of American military
power. Formulation of this policy commitment began seven
months before hostilities with Spain; it began with Presidential
examination of a Navy Department memorandum authored by
Assistant Secretary Theodore Roosevelt. This multi-purpose
paper made one especially bold suggestion: in event of war with
Spain, the Asiatic squadron "should blockade, and if possible
take Manila." Temporarily put in abeyance by a shortlived

détente with Spain in late 1897, the suggestion was revived and made the basis of Roosevelt's famous February 25 orders instructing Commodore George Dewey to "start offensive operations in the Philippines" after eliminating the Spanish fleet. Often viewed simply as a conspiratorial effort by "large policy" extremists, this interpretation misses two more significant facts: first, that Roosevelt's superiors accepted his orders concerning Philippine operations even though they unceremoniously countermanded fully two-thirds of the other miscellaneous orders issued concurrently by the Assistant Secretary; second, that the administration thereafter permitted the Naval War Board to incorporate the February 25 orders into its overall strategy plans for the Pacific. Clearly, while Roosevelt's actions may have been precipitate, they fell within the main lines of the "larger policies" of the administration. Of these, Roosevelt, as he privately admitted, was largely "ignorant."

With the outbreak of war, the McKinley administration rushed to implement its designs upon the likeliest *entrepôt,* Manila, by determining to send an army of occupation to the Philippine capital. It made this decision on May 2 before full-blown rumors of Dewey's victory at Manila Bay reached Washington, and formally issued the call for Philippine volunteers on May 4, three days before an anxious Navy Department received authoritative word that the Asiatic squadron was safe. The determined size of the army force was to be "not less than twenty thousand men"—four times the number recommended by Dewey "to retain (Manila) and thus control the Philippine Islands."

On May 11, McKinley and his cabinet gave definite form to American aims by approving a State Department memorandum calling for Spanish cession of a suitable "coaling station," presumably Manila. The islands as a whole were to remain with Spain. Shortly thereafter, on June 3, when it had become apparent that the great distance between Manila and Honolulu demanded an intermediate coaling and cable station, the President broadened the American position to include an island in the Marianas. The choice made was Guam, and the United States Navy promptly seized it.

As of early June, then, administration intent envisioned only postwar control of Manila and Guam as way stations to the Orient. But dramatic events swiftly undercut this limited resolve and, for a critical fortnight, set American policy aimlessly adrift upon uncertain seas. First of all, the emergence of the Philippine insurgents as "an important factor" crystallized administration belief (as one American diplomat later noted), that "Spain cannot control; if we evacuate, anarchy rules." What then; bestow the largess of Philippine independence? The mere posing of the alternative raised an even more threatening specter of European intervention against a weak, fledging republic, an intervention warned against by American diplomats in Berlin and Paris and lent specific credibility by German actions and attitudes. Either possibility—nationalistic revolution or rival intervention—might well render the isolated American position in Manila less than useful. . . .

Cognizant of this, the McKinley administration, in mid-June, made a determined effort to break the bind by initiating three dramatic and interrelated moves in Hawaii, China, and the Philippines designed to increase American influence in the Western Pacific.

On June 11, the administration reactivated the sagging debate on Hawaiian annexation in the hope of strengthening America's hand in the Pacific basin. In the ensuing congressional debate, administration spokesmen hammered one theme with greater constancy than others: "we must have Hawaii to help us get our share of China." America, so the argument went, needed Hawaii not only for its own economic or cultural worth, but also for its commercial and military value as a stepping-stone to the China market. . . .

Significantly, anti-annexationists did not dispute the desirability of commercial expansion into Asia. Some even admitted the necessity of commercial-military bases as accoutrements to this expansion, but argued that the Pearl Harbor lease of 1886 or the Kiska holding in the Aleutians already met such needs. Most, however, stressed the laissez faire, free trade approach that "commercial expansion" could best be realized "by competition of quality and price," not by "annexation of territory." The point did not carry. On June 15, the House passed the annexation resolution by an overwhelming vote, 209 to 91. Three weeks later, after redundant and desultory discussion, the Senate affirmed the measure by a similar ratio. Thus, on July 8, with McKinley's signature, America acquired her halfway house to the Orient. The acquisition followed by four days the occupation of Wake Island, a move intended to meet the technological necessities of an additional cable point between Hawaii and Guam.

Synchronous with the push on Hawaiian annexation, the administration initiated the first step in an American economic offensive in China itself by proposing a government commercial commission to China to recommend measures for trade expansion. Secretary of State William R. Day's supporting letter to Congress made it pointedly clear that the internal economic situation necessitated a vigorous commercial expansion in China. Declaring that an industrial production "of large excess above the demands of home consumption" demanded "an enlargement of foreign markets," the Secretary concluded that "nowhere is this consideration of more interest than in its relation to the Chinese Empire." Aware that "the partition of commercial facilities" in China threatened America's "important interests," he still contended that "the United States . . . is in a position to invite the most favorable concessions to its industries and trade . . . provided the conditions are thoroughly understood and proper advantage is taken of the present situation." Congress, to be sure, failed to appropriate the necessary monies. The reason, significantly, was because it considered such one-shot missions an inadequate substitute for a thoroughgoing reform of our consular representation in China. Nevertheless, the administration proposal, coupled with intensified consular activities later in the summer, served clear notice of American intent to take "proper advantage . . . of the present situation" in order to play a more active role in China.

Simultaneously, on June 14, the administration capped its trio of dramatic moves by shelving the earlier decision to return the Philippines to Spain, thus opening the disposition of the islands to further examination. With this open-ended shift, there began a progressive but reluctant redefinition of the desired area of American sovereignty; from Manila, to Luzon, and finally to the entire group. For two months after the June 14 move, American policy remained seemingly ambivalent on the question of extent. Even the Armistice agreement of August appeared to avoid confrontation of the issue by reserving the question of "control, disposition, and government" for final peace negotiations. The ambiguity was more apparent than real, for McKinley had already crushed an internal move headed by his own secretary of state to limit American commitment to Manila. In sealing this extremity, he left open only the question of how far to journey toward the other—Luzon or the entire group? The beginning of the final negotiations in early October found this problem still unresolved. While the American peace commissioners were instructed to work only for retention of Luzon, they were also to "accumulate all possible information" on the possible necessity of controlling the whole archipelago. Less than one month later, on October 25, McKinley himself finally cut the knot by broadening his instructions to include all the Philippines.

In this evolution of Philippine policy, America's commercial stake in China was of considerable importance. Indeed, it played the primary role in the thinking of the business and government elite that chiefly shaped McKinley's decisions. It also played a significant though not paramount, part in the outlook of the military advisers who exercised a more limited but still crucial influence upon the President's policies.

Between June and October, business and government circles united vigorously around a policy of retaining all or part of the Philippines. Significantly, their rationale stressed the intrinsic economic worth of the islands far less than their strategic relationship to China—both as a commercial *entrepôt* and a political-military lever. Moreover, it emphasized that Manila alone would not suffice for these purposes; that the United States would have to take Luzon and perhaps the whole group. In part this support for enlarged control reflected the pervading fear that native revolution or European penetration might undermine the viability of American power in Manila. It also indicated a growing belief, born of newly accumulated information, that the economic interdependence of the archipelago made efficient division most difficult. . . .

Numerous business associations, as well as prominent individual businessmen, pushed the viewpoint that trade interests in China demanded American control in the Philippines. Led by the National Association of Manufacturers and the American Asiatic Association, many special business organizations urged retention of the Philippines "for the protection and furtherance of the commercial interests of our citizens in the Far East." At the same time, save for a few prominent dissenters, McKinley's many personal friends in the corporate world gave similar counsel. . . .

Most of McKinley's close associates in the government (many of whom were themselves products of the business community) pressed similar views upon their chief. The redoubtable Mark Hanna, State Department economic expert Frederic Emory, the American Minister to China Charles Denby, his successor Edwin H. Conger, Comptroller of The Currency Charles C. Dawes, Assistant Secretary of The Treasury Frank A. Vanderlip, to name a few, all shared in general the conviction, (as Vanderlip stated) that an American-controlled Philippines would be "pickets of the Pacific, standing guard at the entrances to trade with the millions of China and Korea, French Indo-China, the Malay Peninsula, and the island of Indonesia."

Exerting a more narrow influence upon McKinley's Philippine policy was a third group, the military. In general, the President's military advisers shared the widespread concern over the strategic relationship of the archipelago to the Asian mainland. Yet, attracted by the siren's call of *imperium* (in which they would play a prominent role), many military spokesmen also promoted retention of the Philippines as the first step toward an expansive territorial imperialism. In the main, their hopes were dashed as McKinley refused to heed their advice for a general American expansion into Micronesia and the islands of the South China Sea. Military advice, however, could claim one significant result: it resolved the President's ambivalence (shared by the business and government elite) between taking Luzon or the entire group by convincing him that the islands were an indivisible entity: that strategically and economically they were highly interdependent. Especially persuasive were the lengthy and articulate reports of Commander R. B. Bradford and General Francis V. Greene. Coming in late September and early October, they proved to be the decisive factors in broadening the President's instructions to their ultimate dimensions.

The great repute of these business and government groups, coupled with their ready access to the Chief Executive, gave much weight to their contention (shared, in part, by the military) that American interests in China necessitated retention of the Philippines. But this view also gained a powerful though unwanted ally in the twin crisis in China itself during the fall of 1898. One side of the crisis was the intensified partitioning of railroad concessions by the European powers. Begun in the aftermath of the Sino-Japanese War, the division of concession spheres had advanced greatly by late summer of 1898. Russia and Germany had established *de facto* monopolization of Manchurian and Shantung railroads, respectively, while England bent her own efforts to strengthening her hold in the Yangtze Valley. British acceptance of the modified Open Door policy and the ratification of the Anglo-German railroad accord of September showed unmistakably that the Open Door had no current relevance to the world of railroad investments. From the American point of view, the development augured ill for its own economic interests. To be sure, it did not greatly injure American investors. At this stage there was still little American financial interest in Chinese investments; and what little existed was assured profitable employment by the British in the Yangtze Valley. The solidification of railroad spheres, however, did threaten the important American export trade of Manchuria and North China by requiring American goods to travel from treaty port to market over Russian and German railroads. The prospect was not inviting, for these products might well meet railroad rate discrimination which, in raising transportation costs, would render American articles less competitive.

Meanwhile, America's economic dreams faced another menace from a different quarter in China. In September of 1898, a successful coup d'etat by conservative, anti-foreign elements managed to crush the pro-western, reform party surrounding the young Chinese Emperor. The new government immediately initiated administrative measures viewed by the United States as inimical to "commercial development" and the "pendulum of progress." More seriously, the conservative forces failed to control anti-foreign uprisings inspired by their own *putsch*. Centered along projected Manchurian railroads, the violent and unstabilizing demonstrations offered both the excuse and the opportunity for potential Russian intervention to save her great railroad interests. The mere suggestion of such a development was sufficient to conjure up visions of a further fragmented China and a vitiated Open Door.

These developments in China spawned first alarm, then action in the McKinley administration. The first move came in September with official renewal of inquiries to Russia and Germany concerning trade policies in their respective spheres. While the German response seems satisfactory, the evasive Russian declaration that her "administrative regulations" on foreign trade were still undetermined appear to be a foreboding retreat from earlier positions. Thus accentuated, State Department concern germinated a second move in October with favorable action upon a textile industry petition concerning the Russian threat in China. Noting that one-half of America's cotton textile exports to China went to Russian-dominated areas, the petitioners demanded a "vigorous policy" to prevent "these markets" from being "eventually closed to our trade." Immediately, the Department responded by instructing its embassy in St. Petersburg to "use every opportunity to act energetically" against Russian adoption of discriminatory trade policies in Manchuria. Quite obviously, the American government regarded the crises in China as dangerous enough to warrant substantial American reaction. Presumably, the situation was sufficiently threatening to impart added urgency and impact to the already influential opinion that America's commercial aspirations in China necessitated retention of the Philippines.

There can be no doubt that the Chinese question, illuminated by the opinion of business, government, and the military and by the growing crises in China, had progressive impact upon the shaping of America's Philippine policy. Nowhere is that fact made more significantly and dramatically apparent than in the private, candid, and lengthy exchange of opinions between McKinley and his peace commissioners at a White House meeting on September 16. The President, speaking somberly and with none of his frequent evasiveness, explained his reasons for retaining all or part of the archipelago. Almost all of them were negative, embraced with obvious reluctance. The only positive and assertive determinant was his conviction that "our tenure in the Philippines" offered the "commercial opportunity" of maintaining the Open Door, a policy which McKinley defined as "no advantages in the Orient which are not common to all." "Asking only the open door for ourselves," he told his commissioners, "we are ready to accord the open door to others." Explaining further, he made it clear that retention was no first step in an orgy of imperialism and jingoism, but simply a limited though important accoutrement to commercial expansion. "The commercial opportunity . . . associated with this opening," he declared, "depends less on large territorial possessions than upon an adequate commercial basis and upon broad and equal privileges." The statement was more than rhetoric. Before the conclusion of peace, McKinley was to turn his back on jingoistic pressure to acquire all the Carolines and the Marianas from Spain, thus further illustrating that commercial needs, not Manifest Destiny, guided American decision-making in the Pacific basin; that the Open Door, not colonialism on a vast scale, was to remain the vehicle of American expansion. . . .

The grand scheme was not, in the narrow sense, imperial. The insular possessions in the Pacific were not pieces of empire, per se, but stepping-stones and levers to be utilized upon a larger and more important stage—China. Paradoxically, American expansion was designed, in part, to serve an anti-imperial purpose of preventing the colonization of China and thus preserving her for Open Door market penetration: *imperium in anti-imperio*. All this McKinley captured in his presidential message of December 5, 1898, when he declared that our "vast commerce . . . and the necessity of our staple production for Chinese uses" had made the United States a not "indifferent spectator of the extraordinary" partitioning in China's maritime provinces. Nevertheless, he continued, so long as "no discriminatory treatment of American . . . trade be found to exist . . . the need for our country becoming an actor in the scene" would be "obviated." But, he concluded, the fate of the Open Door would not be left to chance; it would be, he stated, "my aim to subserve our large interests in that quarter by all means appropriate to the constant policy of our government." Quite obviously, the fruits of the Spanish-American War had enormously multiplied the "appropriate ... means" available to American policy-makers, and had set the stage for the illusory search of America for that holy commercial grail—the China market.

* * * *

14   *Teodoro A. Agoncillo*

The Filipino Point of View

Teodoro A. Agoncillo (1900–   ) is the grandson of Felipe Agoncillo, Emilio Aguinaldo's special emissary to President McKinley and the Paris Peace Commission during the trying days (for the Filipinos) of 1898–1899. Since the end of World War II the younger Agoncillo has been one of several Filipino scholars engaged in researching and writing a multivolume history of the movement for Philippine independence. In 1958, the United States government, as an act of intellectual friendship, transferred the 400,000 items in the Philippine Insurgent Records from the National Archives in Washington to the Filipino government. This greatly facilitated the work on Agoncillo's volume, which covers the period from 1896 to 4 July 1902 (the date of Theodore Roosevelt's amnesty proclamation to the Filipino insurgents). Though marred by a bitter anticlerical stance and a pardonable anti-American bias, this volume is still important for the light it sheds on Aguinaldo's repeated efforts (through Agoncillo and others) to effect a working diplomatic relationship with the McKinley Administration in 1898. On the other hand, compare the interpretation of Bryan's role in the treaty fight with the subsequent selection by Paolo E. Coletta.

As early as June 10, 1898, Agoncillo wrote Aguinaldo that a representative be sent to the United States in order to ascertain American intentions regarding the Philippines. Owing perhaps

SOURCE. Teodoro A. Agoncillo, *Malolos: The Crisis of the Republic,* Quezon City: University of the Philippines Press, 1960, pp. 310–372 *passim.* Reprinted by permission of the publisher and the author.

to this suggestion, the decree of June 23 provided for the creation of a committee to take charge of what may properly be called a propaganda corps. On August 7, Aguinaldo instructed Agoncillo to publish the "Act of Proclamation" and the "Manifesto to Foreign Governments" in the Hong Kong papers. Furthermore, he exhorted Agoncillo to exert all efforts in publicizing the Philippine situation, adding:

"It is important that you should go (to the United States) as soon as possible, so that McKinley's Government would know the true situation. Show him that our people have their own Government, civil organizations in the provinces already exist, and soon the Congress of Representatives of these provinces will meet. Tell him that they cannot do with the Philippines what they like.... ***The policy that you will pursue in the United States is as follows: make them understand that whatever might be their intentions toward us it will not be possible for them to overrule the sentiments of the people represented by the government and so it cannot be ignored by them.... Still, do not accept any contracts or give any promises respecting protection or annexation, because we shall see first if we can obtain independence. That is what we shall secure in the meantime, if it should be possible to do so. ***Give them to understand in a way that you are unable to obligate yourself, but once we are independent then we shall be able to make arrangements with them."

Three days later, on August 10, Aguinaldo once more wrote Agoncillo urging him to proceed at once to the United States to represent the country there....

In view of Aguinaldo's eagerness in inaugurating a "diplomatic" offensive, Agoncillo, on August 26, wrote that he needed his credentials immediately as representative to the United States and suggested that two or three representatives be sent to the United States in order to form a diplomatic mission. At the same time, he pointed out that it was doubtful whether Japan could be relied upon by the Filipinos in their struggle for recognition, for he believed that Japan and England had an understanding regarding the Philippine question in the event that other Powers interfered with the Americans in the Philippines.

Help from Japan, therefore, could not be expected as long as the United States was in the Philippines.

In what may be regarded as final instructions to Agoncillo, Aguinaldo, on August 30, wrote:

"It is said that General Merritt is going away to take part in the work of the Commission (Paris Peace Conference). On this account, it is important that you proceed as quickly as possible to America, in order to know what will take place. If perchance we should go back to Spanish control, ask them (the Americans) to help us as the French helped them during their own revolution and ask also the terms. . . . In whatever agreement you will make you will insert as a condition the recognition of this government. . . ."

Armed with Aguinaldo's instructions as contained in the letters dated August 7 and 30, and some 16,000 pesos, Agoncillo boarded the steamer *China* on September 2, bound for the United States. With him was his *comprovinciano* and secretary, Sixto Lopez. . . .

Agoncillo took advantage of the presence of General Francis V. Greene on the steamer *China* to confer with him on matters pertaining to the Philippines. Greene impliedly expressed his doubt as to the ability of the Filipinos to sustain an independent government. Agoncillo, however, assured him that they could and added that he thought the free nations of the world who considered themselves the torchbearers of civilization and symbols of justice would recognize an independent Philippines. As a reminder, he pointed out that the Filipinos did exactly what the Americans did when they threw off the British yoke. If so, why, then, should the United States and other free nations deny to the Filipinos their right to be free and independent? He convinced Greene that the Filipinos had their own civilization and were better off than the Cubans. The result of this conversation was that Greene, upon their arrival in San Francisco, informed the American people, through the press, of what Agoncillo had told him.

The ship docked in San Francisco on September 22. Since it had been known in the United States and in Europe that

Agoncillo left Hong Kong on his way to America, the Americans, in their staggering ignorance of geography, expected that he would arrive on civilized American soil naked, except for the G-strings. They were, however, dumbfounded to see a highly educated man, complete with hat and well-pressed European suit, go down the gangplank with superior airs. On the same day, he and Greene took the train for Washington, D.C., where they arrived on September 27. It was during this land journey to the American capital that Agoncillo learned from the news-papers that he would not be officially received by Washington. He then requested Greene to make arrangements with President McKinley in order to confer with him officially. Greene, an understanding and accommodating man, did so upon their arrival in Washington, but the President expressed his regret that he could not see Agoncillo officially because it would be contrary to American understanding with Spain. However, he expressed his willingness to see Agoncillo unofficially. Disap-pointed, Agoncillo then sounded out the State Department re-garding the acceptance of his credentials. He was met with a rebuff. At this point, he took it upon himself to see President McKinley at 10:00 A.M. on October 1. He was politely received in the official reception room. Agoncillo recounted to McKinley the Filipinos' struggles to be free. Although the President lis-tened politely it was obvious that Agoncillo's mission to the United States was bound to fail. He then asked McKinley if he would be allowed to state the aims and purposes of the Philippine Government. McKinley answered that a secret note to this effect should be handed to him, a note, McKinley added, that should be personal and without Agoncillo's official designa-tion. On October 3, Agoncillo handed the note to Assistant Secretary of State Adee, who in turn showed it to the President. The latter instructed Adee to accept Agoncillo's note on condition that he would agree to some amendments. Agoncillo, after conferring with Adee and learning that insistence on acceptance of his official note might result in its total rejection, gracefully accepted the amendments. The note, in its final form, reviewed the background of the Filipino-American relations, and then continued:

"...The present lawful Philippine Government of which the invincible leader General Emilio Aguinaldo is the president, also believes that the moment has come to remind and even notify, if proper, in a formal and precise manner, the Illustrious President and Government of Washington of its existence and normal and regular functioning, as well as of its relations of reciprocity with the authorities of the American Republic in the Philippine Islands.

It desires to state (in the same manner), that the Philippine people unanimously confirms its independence and confides that the American people will recognize the same, mindful of the offers made and obligations contracted in its name, proclaiming the principles of liberty, justice and right expressed in its famous, sacred Declaration of Independence for the benefit of the new nation which logically rises in that part of the globe under the impulse of its present beneficent and humanitarian action.

And the Philippine people hope that pending a permanent understanding for the evacuation of their territory, their present lawful *de facto* government will be accorded the rights of a belligerent and such other rights as may be proper, in order to compel Spain to submit to the just historical law which deprives her of the tutelage she has arrogated to herself over those Islands and which she was incapable of carrying on humanely and socially without detriment to the general interests...."

It was then agreed that Agoncillo's note be sent to the American commissioners in Paris. Agoncillo was further advised to hurry thither in order to have an interview with the commissioners. It is apparent that official Washington wanted to get rid of him in order to free itself from the possible embarrassment of dealing with the representative of the Philippine Government that the United States had no intention of recognizing. But Agoncillo thought that such show of assumed or studied sympathy was an invitation for the Philippines to send a representative to the Commission in Paris. While he thought that many Americans were for Philippine independence, yet Agoncillo clearly saw that he was fighting a lost cause and warned Aguinaldo that the people should be prepared for a possible conflict with the Americans....

The deliberations of the Commissioners were closely followed by the Filipino agents abroad, particularly by Agoncillo whose duty it was to present before the conference the Filipino side of the Philippine question. As the deliberations dragged on and Agoncillo was not given a chance to air his views, the agents in Europe and in Hong Kong came to the conclusion that there was nothing more to do than to wait for developments. Agoncillo, however, upon learning of the conclusion of the treaty, submitted a memorandum to the Peace Commissioners, through General Greene, in which he said that the treaty "cannot be accepted as binding by my government inasmuch as the commission did not hear the Filipino people or admit them into its deliberations, when they have the undisputable right to intervene in all that might affect their future life." The commission merely shrugged its shoulders and ignored Agoncillo's protest. Agoncillo, as early as December 1, had admitted that the Philippines would be annexed to the United States. In view of Agoncillo's failure to be heard in the Paris conference, Ramon Abarca, treasurer of the Filipino Republican Committee of Paris, telegraphed Apacible on December 14 proposing the immediate return of Agoncillo to Washington. It was felt that Agoncillo's only hope was in preventing the ratification of the treaty by the American Senate.

At the point when all seemed lost and when the Filipino leaders sensed the inevitability of an armed conflict with the Americans, they proposed a Filipino-Spanish alliance in order to fight the new enemy. The weakness of Spain's economy and international position, what with the war in Cuba sapping her resources and the reluctance of the European concert to intervene in Cuban affairs on behalf of Spain, obviously encouraged the Filipino leaders to take advantage of the situation to force Spain to deal with them directly. Most of Luzon was in the hands of the rebels; the Visayas was seething; and the Spanish forces in Mindanao were floundering helplessly with no hope of aid either from Manila or from Spain. With thousands of Spaniards taken prisoner, the rebel leaders tried to strengthen their bargaining power by using the Spanish prisoners as bait. Consequently, they advanced the following propositions as *modus vivendi*: (1) the conclusion of an agreement of peace and friendship between the Philippines and Spain as soon as the Philippines was recognized; (2) the renunciation by the Philippines and Spain of any claim to public and private property; (3) the grant to Spain of the most-favored nation right; (4) the payment of 7,000,000 pesos to the Philippine Government; (5) the cession to the Philippines of the Carolines and the Marianas; (6) the prohibition by Spain for the friars to go to the Philippines; and (7) the renunciation by the Spanish friars of all claims to property in the Philippines and their departure from the country within forty-five days. Evidently, none of the Spaniards took the proposition seriously.

Aguinaldo, realizing the hopelessness of fighting for the recognition of an independent Philippines, now appealed to McKinley, proposing (1) that the Spanish possessions in Oceania be formed into a state and named "Republic of the Philippines" under the protection of the United States; (2) that the purpose of the protectorate under the United States was to make Spain abandon her possessions in Oceania and, too, to make the United States work for the recognition of the Republic by the foreign Powers; (3) that a commission composed of Filipinos and Americans be created to determine the period of protectorate and to formulate a treaty of alliance between the Philippines and the United States. McKinley, however, had no need for such an ambitious alliance, for he had (long since) made up his mind that the Philippines should belong to the United States.

Back in Washington, Sixto Lopez, Agoncillo's secretary, wrote the Secretary of State, on January 5, 1899, asking that Agoncillo be given an audience in order "to arrange for the presentation of his letter of credentials to the President of the United States." In view of the recent events, he urged the advisability of an "understanding between the American Government and the representative of the Philippine people as to the relation between the respective nations." Hay conveniently ignored Lopez's letter. It was at this time that General Otis, who had so sanguinely assured the War Department that the Philippine situation was well in hand, wrote Washington communicating his pessimistic prognostications that the mounting strained relations between the rebels and the American troops bode ill for the future. McKinley, who had a sincere desire to avert any

unnecessary trouble with the rebels, called in General Greene
on January 10 and ask[ed] him to work on Agoncillo, who was
apparently close to the General, with a view to making him sign
a prepared telegram to Aguinaldo asking the latter to prevent the
outbreak of hostilities between the allies. Greene conferred
with Secretary Hay, and the first draft of the proposed telegram
to be sent by Agoncillo to Aguinaldo was prepared. McKinley
changed the wording of the telegram, the final draft then reading:

"Nothing would be so unfortunate for the Filipinos as a conflict with the United States. Hasty or inconsiderate action now
would only delay the realization of our hopes for generations.
You should know that nothing can be done for us until the
sovereignty of the United States is recognized. I am firmly convinced that the United States have no motive but our good and
want to be our friends and not our enemies."

Greene promptly translated the telegram into Spanish and
hurried to the Arlington Hotel to see Agoncillo. Probably upon
instructions of McKinley or Hay or both, Greene told Agoncillo
that an armed conflict with the Americans would be disastrous
to the Filipinos and would result in mutual hatred. Then he
pressured Agoncillo to send the prepared telegram to Aguinaldo,
adding that it was now within his powers to avert a crisis. Tears
gleamed in Agoncillo's eyes as he listened patiently to Greene's
exhortations, but he told Greene frankly that he would not do
such a thing. He was, he added, powerless to prevent any outbreak of hostilities and only the recognition of Philippine independence would satisfy the Filipinos. The contents of the telegram constituted, he said, a betrayal of the Philippine cause and
its effects would be a burden on his conscience. No, he would
not sign the telegram. Greene alternately cajoled and threatened,
and made the promise that the United States would work for
the welfare of the Philippines. Adamantly, Agoncillo stood his
ground and reminded Greene that such a course of action as
was contemplated in the telegram would mean the end of his
career. Greene left the Arlington empty-handed. . . .
    Meanwhile, the American Senate was girding for a final show-

down on the ratification of the Paris treaty. On January 25, the Senate, on motion of Senator Davis, unanimously agreed to vote on the treaty on February 6. It was evident that the Republicans would not be able to muster the necessary two-thirds majority to make the treaty effective. Unfortunately, however, William Jennings Bryan, the defeated Democratic candidate for the Presidency in 1896 whom H. L. Mencken denounced as "a charlatan, a mountebank, a zany without sense or dignity," suddenly turned about and urged his Democratic colleagues to vote for the treaty. Bryan was playing politics when he based his betrayal on the dubious assumption that the issue of imperialism could and would be leveled against the Republicans in the next elections. . . .

Bryan's sudden switch to the imperialist side precisely to confront the Republicans with the issue of imperialism in the next elections definitely contributed to the swelling of the number of the proponents of the treaty. One other factor, perhaps the most crucial, was the unfortunate breaking out of the Filipino-American hostilities at the psychological moment. The incident was used by the imperialists to point out that the Filipinos were guilty of firing the first shot. Thus, those who were at first against the ratification of the treaty changed their stand two days before the voting. Their suspicion that the Filipinos began the hostilities was magnified when Agoncillo, on February 5, quietly fled to Montreal, Canada. The treaty was ratified on February 6 by a vote of sixty-one to twenty-nine.

Even when Agoncillo was already beyond American jurisdiction, his assassination was attempted on orders of some "patriotic" Americans who mistook his flight for dear life as evidence of his complete knowledge of the outbreak of the Filipino-American hostilities which, as he stated in his previous letters to Secretary Hay, he feared might break out. To escape persecution, he boarded a steamer for Europe, but unfortunately the ship was wrecked off the coast of New Foundland and all the documents he had with him were lost. . . .

The news of the annexation of the Philippines to the United States was received in the country with mixed feelings. To the vested interests, the Treaty of Paris was a wish fulfilled; to the idealistic patriots and nationalists, the news was the harbinger of dark days to come. In Pasig, the residents passed a resolution expressing their loyalty to the Philippine Government and to Aguinaldo and offering their lives in the interest of the country's freedom. Resolutions protesting the annexation of the Philippines to the United States were passed by the residents of Navotas, Pateros, San Pedro Makati, San Felipe Neri, then in Manila Province; by the people of Ilocos Sur, Batanes, Tayabas, Albay, Camarines, Zambales, Samar, Ilocos Norte, Cagayan, Cavite, Pampanga, Capiz, Pangasinan, and other places such as Malibay (now in Pasay), Sampaloc, San Mateo, Las Piñas, Antipolo, San Miguel (Manila), Tondo, and Kalumpit. It was obvious that the people, as distinguished from the intelligentsia and the wealthy, were for continuing the struggle for freedom and independence.

PART FOUR

The Protest Against Imperialism

THE PROTEST
AGAINST IMPERIALISM

15   *Fred H. Harrington*

The Anti-Imperialists: Too Few, Too Feeble

Educated at Cornell and New York University (Ph.D., 1937), Fred H. Harrington (1912–   ) was for many years a very influential teacher of American diplomatic history at Wisconsin before becoming its president in 1962. Harrington is commonly regarded as the dominant academic influence in shaping the thinking of William A. Williams and the younger disciples of the so-called "Wisconsin school" of American diplomatic history. Though published in 1935, this article is still the standard initial reference for anyone seeking a fuller understanding of anti-imperialist thought and action during this period. Note how Harrington, the historical pragmatist, condemns these idealists (and some neorealists) for their collective impotence.

On May 1, 1898, the Asiatic Squadron of the United States Navy, under the command of Commodore George Dewey, engaged and virtually annihilated a Spanish fleet at anchor under the batteries of Cavite in Manila Bay. This victory, which gave the United States the first foothold in the Philippines, marks a turning point in the history of American territorial expansion.

SOURCE. Fred Harvey Harrington, "The Anti-Imperialist Movement in the United States, 1898–1900," in *Mississippi Valley Historical Review*, XXII (September, 1935), pp. 211–230. Reprinted by permission of the publisher and the author.

It marks as well the beginning of a protest movement of proportions, a movement led by a strangely assorted group of citizens who fought renunciation of the spoils of war. Although it failed to achieve its purposes, the movement is of importance, for it held the political stage in the United States for two full years, and attracted to its ranks such public men as Bryan and Cleveland, Reed and Carnegie, Schurz and Hoar.

In approaching the anti-imperialist movement, it is well to bear in mind that it was based almost exclusively on grounds of abstract political principle. The anti-imperialists did not oppose colonial expansion for commercial, religious, constitutional, or humanitarian reasons. They opposed it because they thought that an imperialist policy ran counter to the political doctrines of the Declaration of Independence, Washington's Farewell Address, and Lincoln's Gettysburg Address—the doctrines which asserted that a government could not rule peoples without their consent, and that the United States, having been conceived as an instrument of and for its own people, should not imitate the methods or interfere in the affairs of the Old World nations in any way.

However these doctrines may be regarded today, there can be no doubt that they had a very real meaning for the citizens who organized the anti-imperialist movement. Almost to a man the anti-expansionists sincerely believed that abandonment of these "guiding principles" would mean the doom of the republic. This feeling was reflected time after time in articles, speeches, and private correspondence of the leaders. It was proclaimed in the utterances of Carl Schurz, David Starr Jordan, William Jennings Bryan, Grover Cleveland, and Thomas B. Reed—men who represented five distinct groups in the movement. . . .

David Starr Jordan, one of the first of many educators to declare against expansion, voiced the same sentiment when he told a San Francisco audience that to hold Cuba or the Philippines as colonies, "our democracy must necessarily depart from its best principles and traditions." "There was a great danger . . . ," he thought, "that in easy victory we might lose sight of the basal principles of the Republic, a cooperative association in which 'all just government is derived from the consent of the governed'."

Nor were the words of the two great Democratic leaders different in language or tone. "Our guns destroyed a Spanish fleet,"
Bryan told an Omaha audience on June 14, "but can they destroy
that self-evident truth, that governments derive their just powers,
not from superior force, but from the consent of the governed?"
Just a week later, in an address at Lawrenceville, New Jersey,
Cleveland asserted that "our government was formed for the
express purpose of creating in a new world a new nation, the
foundation of which should be man's self-government," and that
to embark on a career of colonial aggrandizement would be to
"abandon . . . old landmarks and to follow the lights of mon-
archical hazards."

Speaker Reed, the most prominent Republican to oppose expansion, made no public pronouncement on the subject. In
private, however, he let it be known that he would not support
his party in opposing the "foundation principles of our government."

It can readily be seen that, in each instance, the whole weight
of the argument is made to rest on the point of political principle.
This is the case with the other anti-imperialist speeches as well.
It is true that, in the later phases on the movement, economic,
constitutional, military, and humanitarian arguments were advanced against expansion, but they were used to supplement the
fundamental conception. Even after the Philippine atrocities
had caused many anti-expansionists to stress the humanitarian
aspects of their case, the leaders continued to regard the question
of political ideals as the real basis for their opposition to a
colonial policy.

The anti-imperialist movement began to take shape almost
immediately after the Battle of Manila Bay, as a protest against
the wave of expansion sentiment set in motion by Dewey's
victory. Expansionists were clamoring for the annexation of
Hawaii and the "retention" of the Philippines. Whitelaw Reid's
New York *Tribune* was declaring editorially that "this country
will be bound, in honor and in morals, either itself to assume
the administration of the islands or to empower some other
competent authority to do so," even before the news of the
naval victory had been confirmed. Other papers—the bulk of
the administration press and some Democratic organs—followed

the *Tribune's* lead, declaring for expansion on military, religious, commercial, humanitarian, and other grounds.

Those opposed to imperialism immediately took the field in reply. They came forward as individuals, with statements similar to those quoted above, and made themselves heard through the press. From the start they enlisted the services of the independent Democratic and Mugwump press—papers like the New York *Evening Post,* the Springfield *Republican,* the Boston *Herald,* and the Baltimore *Sun.* These papers became the mainstays of the anti-imperialist support, but they were by no means alone in their denunciation of expansion. Many regular Democratic journals—the Chicago *Chronicle,* the Kansas City *Times,* the Charleston *News and Courier,* and the Richmond *Times,* to name but a few—followed the lead of Bryan or Cleveland in opposing imperialism. They were joined by a few Republican organs of independent leanings, among them the Boston *Transcript,* the Philadelphia *Ledger,* and the Pittsburgh *Dispatch.*

Despite this support, the anti-imperialist movement achieved no satisfactory organization in the early months of its existence. War feeling was still running high. It was as yet uncertain what the policy of the administration would be. And, most important of all, there was no feeling of common purpose among those opposed to a colonial policy. Cleveland and Bryan, though both anti-imperialists and both Democrats, had no love for each other, and their forces were not disposed to cooperate on short notice even in the face of common danger. Reed and Hoar and the other regular Republicans who feared expansion, recoiled at the thought of associating with Schurz and the other Mugwumps.

Thus handicapped, the anti-imperialists made slow progress at first. They were able to put up little opposition to the annexation of Hawaii, which the most prominent anti-imperialist organ termed a "letting out of the waters," the first step in a definitely imperialistic policy. Henry Cabot Lodge, leader of the imperialists in Congress, could dismiss the first large anti-imperialist meeting as one of the "comic incidents" of the war, and the Saratoga Conference, which was organized by Carl Schurz to impress on President McKinley the dangers of expansion, actually delivered itself into the hands of the enemy.

Organization, however, came in time. By the time of the cessation of hostilities, it had become reasonably certain that the administration would adopt an imperialist policy. Those opposed to expansion began to realize the absolute necessity of common action. The independents, convinced that anti-imperialism took precedence over all other reforms, led the way. In Boston, under Gamaliel Bradford and Moorfield Storey, two Mugwumps, they organized a non-partisan Committee of Correspondence, designed to unite workers for the cause irrespective of political faith. Elsewhere they showed a willingness to cooperate with anti-imperialists of every political faith. As time went on, the Bryan and Cleveland Democrats found that the issue might serve as a basis for a mutual understanding, and even the Republicans in the movement—strong party men most of them—displayed a tendency to draw closer to the other opponents of expansion. By January, 1899, George F. Hoar, who had called the Mugwumps the "vilest set of political assassins that ever disgraced this or any other country," was carrying on a close personal correspondence with two Mugwump leaders, Schurz and Storey. Andrew Carnegie, an anti-imperialist to whom the name of Bryan had been anathema two years before, was wishing the Nebraskan "godspeed" and warmly offering him "the hand of fellowship in the new issue before us."

It was this growing sense of common purpose that made possible the formation of the Anti-Imperialist Leagues in the months after November, 1898—leagues that included in their membership most of the prominent opponents of expansion, yet managed to carry on their work without too much internal friction.

The first Anti-Imperialist League, like the earlier Committee of Correspondence, was brought into being by the Boston anti-imperialists. The Bostonians retained control of the executive committee, but membership was open to "any citizen of the United States, irrespective of party . . . if in sympathy with the objects of the League." The forty-one vice-presidents were drawn from all sections of the country.

An examination of the lists of officers of this league and similar organizations (such as the New York Anti-Imperialist League) gives insight into the elements that were behind the anti-imperialist movement. In reviewing these lists, which contain the names of many of the nation's outstanding men, one is struck at first by the heterogeneous character of the league membership. A closer inspection serves to group most of the men into a few quite definite categories, the reformers, the political and economic groups, and the intellectuals.

Unquestionably the most active and enthusiastic of the anti-imperialists were those who had long fought for various political or social reforms. Included in the anti-imperialist movement were representatives of nearly every reform movement prominent in the United States in the second half of the nineteenth century. There were Liberal Republicans of 1872, Mugwumps, civil service enthusiasts—men like Carl Schurz, Charles Francis Adams, E. L. Godkin, Moorfield Storey, Edward Atkinson, and Samuel Bowles. There were municipal reformers—James Coolidge Carter, the Cuttings, and Edward M. Shepard of New York, Edwin Burritt Smith of Chicago, Hazen Pingree of Detroit, George G. Mercer and Herbert Welsh of Philadelphia, and many more. There were social welfare workers, among them Ernest Crosby, Jane Addams, Josephine Lowell, and William Potts. There were single taxers (Crosby, Charles B. Spahr, and Edward Osgood Brown), pacifists (Crosby, Atkinson, and Mercer), Prohibitionists (Senator Edward W. Carmack and John D. White), defenders of Indian rights (Mercer and Welsh), and free traders (Gamaliel Bradford and Albert S. Parsons). The remnant of the old abolition groups, represented by the son of Garrison, the son of Emerson, the son of James Birney, rallied to the cause, as did a number of clergymen, mustering in their ranks Bishop Henry Codman Potter, Henry Van Dyke, Charles H. Parkhurst, Leonard Woolsey Bacon, John White Chadwick, and Theodore Cuyler.

The political elements represented in the movement fall into four distinct groups—the independents, the Gold Democrats, the Bryan Democrats, and the regular Republicans. The independent group, most important of all, need only be mentioned here. It included Schurz, Adams, Storey, Godkin, Bradford, Bowles, Atkinson, and many others, men who have already been mentioned in consideration of their reform activities.

The Gold Democrats also made a notable contribution to the

movement. Headed by ex-President Cleveland himself, the anti-imperialists in this classification numbered most of the prominent Democrats who had bolted Bryan and Free Silver two years before. No less than eight members of Cleveland's Cabinets—Olney, Carlisle, Endicott, Morton, Vilas, Dickinson, Fairchild, and Harmon—came out against expansion, and among the leading anti-imperialists were such Gold Democrats as Bourke Cockran, A. Augustus Healy, Thomas Mott Osborne, Louis Ehrich, and Senator Donelson Caffery.

The Bryan Democrats were significant in the movement for their numbers rather than their leadership. Following Bryan, the majority of the Silverites embraced the anti-imperialist doctrine by 1900, but their advocacy of the cause noticeably lacked the enthusiasm displayed by the independents and the Cleveland men. Only one Bryan Democrat, Senator Ben Tillman, was on the roll of the forty-one vice-presidents of the Anti-Imperialist League, and a mere handful of others, among them Joe Bailey, Champ Clark, and Senator A. O. Bacon, opposed colonial expansion with more than a show of fervor.

The Republicans who joined the anti-imperialist movement were, almost without exception, Republicans of the older generation, former supporters of Frémont and Lincoln who believed they were carrying on the tradition of the party's antislavery days in opposing colonial expansion. They were ably represented in the movement by the president and secretary of the Anti-Imperialist League, George S. Boutwell and Erving Winslow; by Senators Hoar, Hale, and Justin Morrill (who died in December, 1898); by ex-Senators John Sherman, George F. Edmunds, and John B. Henderson, and former President Harrison. Notwithstanding their prominence in party politics, they brought few of the rank and file of the party with them.

A number of Silver Republicans, such as Charles S. Towne and Senator R. F. Pettigrew, a very few Republicans of the younger political generation, among them Henry U. Johnson and Governor William Larrabee, and a scattering of individuals from minor parties also were attracted to the ranks of the anti-imperialists. Few in number, they exercised no important influence on the character of the movement.

Turning from the reform and political classifications, one finds a number of intellectuals in the movement—men who cannot be classified either as reformers or as politicians. They fall into two general categories, the educators and the literary figures. A few college presidents were active anti-imperialists, David Starr Jordan of Stanford and Henry Wade Rogers of Northwestern being the leading examples. Many college professors took the same position, prominent among them being William Graham Sumner, William James, Charles Eliot Norton, Felix Adler, Adolph Cohn, Franklin Henry Giddings, Hermann E. von Holst, William Vaughn Moody, and I. J. McGinity. The literary group contained an equally noteworthy group of men, including Mark Twain, William Dean Howells, Henry B. Fuller, Thomas Wentworth Higginson, Thomas Bailey Aldrich, and Finlay Peter Dunne.

To complete the picture of the anti-imperialist movement, it is necessary to call attention to three economic classifications, the business men and industrialists, the labor leaders, and the "interested groups" in the movement. Though numerically insignificant, each of these groups deserves at least passing mention.

The business and industrial group, very small in size, should be noted because its members, as individuals, did much toward financing the movement. Andrew Carnegie was particularly generous in this respect, and others, including John J. Valentine, Dana Estes, Richard T. Crane, and George Foster Peabody, did their share.

Even smaller was the labor element. The anti-imperialists made great efforts to attract labor support, but, on the whole, were unsuccessful. Samuel Gompers, president of the American Federation of Labor, did show a lively interest in the question, but he was almost the only important labor leader to do so.

Nor did the "interested groups"—the growers of sugar beets, cane sugar, tobacco, and other agricultural products that presumably would suffer from Philippine competition—figure very greatly in the anti-imperialist movement of 1898–1900. Although this may appear surprising in view of the activities of those same groups in the Philippine independence movement thirty years later, it follows from a careful examination of the facts. Two directors of the American Sugar Beet Company were con·

nected with the New York Anti-Imperialist League. At least one farm paper, the *American Agriculturist,* opposed expansion because of the menace of Philippine products. The secretary of the Anti-Imperialist League reported in 1899 that "the tobacco, the beet-sugar and the agricultural interests in general circulated our petitions and made canvasses among their own constituents to bring out remonstrances to the Senate." This, however, is virtually all that can be said of their activities. It does not appear that the "interested groups" contributed much money to the leagues, and certainly they gave the movement few leaders of note. The great majority of the anti-imperialists had no connection, direct or otherwise, with these activities. . . .

The tangible results achieved by the anti-imperialists were few indeed. They may have had some slight influence on the American administration in the islands, by drawing attention to conditions in the Philippines, and, in the course of the long-continued battle for Philippine independence, they may have helped secure the enactment of the Jones Act of 1916. The movement also acted as the agency for restoring many Gold Democrats to party ranks, and for depriving certain Republicans of their influence in the party. But that is all. Beyond these incidental results, the movement seems to have left no perceptible trace in American history. The leaders never gained control of governmental machinery. They did not impress their message on more than a small fraction of the people, and when the Philippine independence bills were finally passed, more than three decades after the second defeat of Bryan, the passage was brought about by a combination of forces very different from those represented in the anti-imperialist movement of 1898–1900.

The reasons for the failure of the anti-imperialist movement are not hard to find. First was the strong position of the imperialists. In the early months of their agitation, the anti-imperialists had to contend with a widespread feeling of nationalism, a feeling engendered by the patriotism and enthusiasm incident to the war with Spain. The people were stirred by the thought of distant possessions, of an empire second to none, a "world power" on whose territories the sun would never set. In time, this feeling gave way to one of indifference, but by then expansion was an accomplished fact.

Second, the anti-imperialists were handicapped by the nature of their case. They were forced to preach abnegation rather than indulgence, to urge the pride of renunciation as against the pride of glory and possession. Their whole case rested on an abstract principle, the application of which was not altogether clear to the public at large. Although they could present a strong emotional argument based on traditions of liberty, the imperialists could more than match this with descriptions of future greatness.

Most tragic of all, however, was the failure to unite in support of a political leader. The majority of the great anti-imperialists —Cleveland and Reed and Hoar are examples—showed no disposition to head a great protest movement. The one available champion of the cause, William Jennings Bryan, was absolutely unacceptable to many anti-imperialists, and was followed by others with extreme reluctance. Men found themselves apologizing rather than fighting for the standard bearer of their cause. And in consequence, what had started as a glorious struggle for freedom ended in bickerings, dissension, and dissatisfaction, a great crusade without crusaders. The anti-imperialists, weakened by desertions and lack of morale, wavered every time they met the enemy, and, in 1900, suffered a rout from which they were never able to recover.

16   *Paolo E. Coletta*

Bryan Was Caught in a Trap

For too many years the most prevalent myth concerning the history of this period was the "fact" that William Jennings Bryan, almost singlehandedly, had been responsible for the Senate approval of the

SOURCE. Paolo E. Coletta, "Bryan, McKinley and the Treaty of Paris." Copyright 1957 by the Pacific Coast Branch, American Historical Association. Reprinted from *Pacific Historical Review*, Vol. XXVI, pp. 131–146, by permission of the Branch.

Treaty of Paris. One of Bryan's contemporaries, Senator George F. Hoar, an anti-expansionist Republican from Massachusetts (who had supported the annexation of Hawaii, but opposed that of the Philippines) went so far as to state in his memoirs that Bryan had switched no less than seventeen Senate votes from opposition to support of the treaty. With minor modifications, this remained the accepted historical view for more than fifty years, until it was challenged by Paolo E. Coletta (1916–   ). A graduate of the University of Missouri (Ph.D., 1942), Professor Coletta has been a member of the faculty at the United States Naval Academy since 1946. In the years 1964–1969 he produced a three-volume life of William Jennings Bryan, which is a model of what political biography ought to be. In this article note Coletta's careful analysis of the treaty vote and the systematic fashion in which he dissipates the theories of an earlier consensus.

One of the commonplaces of history is that the intervention of William Jennings Bryan resulted in the ratification of the Treaty of Paris by the United States Senate. . . . While Bryan did influence a number of senators, approval of the treaty resulted less from his efforts than from an overpowering public demand for colonial expansion and from superb leadership by such Republican senators as Henry Cabot Lodge, Mark Hanna, and Nelson W. Aldrich, including the making of a number of "deals" by which opponents of the treaty were won to its support. . . .

As early as June, 1898, Bryan prayed that a war undertaken in the cause of humanity would not degenerate into one of conquest. "Military lockjaw" kept his ample mouth sealed during the war, but his correspondence indicates that he had a plan to follow once he was discharged from the Army. President William McKinley, meanwhile, undecided with respect to Philippine policy, utterly ignored the question of the government of the Philippines in his annual message of December 3. At that time the administration lacked sufficient strength to ratify the treaty; and Lodge and Theodore Roosevelt, major architects of the "large policy," were plainly worried.

Four schools represent the major divisions of thought on imperialism. Republicans in general favored expansion. Republicans in opposition, led by men like Andrew Carnegie and

Senators George F. Hoar and Walter Mason, would defeat the treaty or amend it by deleting the provision that the United States acquire the Philippines. Democrats in general, and southern Democrats in particular, favored expansion. Bryan headed a minority school that would ratify the treaty in order to end the war, stop the bloodshed, and detach the Philippines from Spain, and then grant the Filipinos independence by congressional resolution.

To Bryan, expansion *per se* was antagonistic to the ideals America had cherished since the days of the Declaration of Independence. Expansion implied that the United States would become involved in the quarrels of Europe and Asia, thereby scrapping the Monroe Doctrine, and in wars for the subjugation of alien races. Most important, colonialism meant the abandonment of the vital principle of government only by the consent of the governed. On these grounds, which reflected his attachment to an isolationist foreign policy and to basic American principles of government, Bryan had ample warrant to oppose ratification. But how could he avoid expansion by supporting a treaty that provided for the acquisition of the Philippines? What appears a dichotomy in his thinking becomes clear upon restatement of his purpose. If the treaty was ratified, Spain would be pushed out of the picture and the United States alone would be in control of Filipino destiny. We would then take the Philippines only long enough to permit the American Congress to resolve that they should be free.

Two days after his discharge from the Army on December 12, Bryan was in Washington demanding that the treaty be approved and that the Congress then resolve upon the nation's policy on expansion, a procedure that made it appear that he had forfeited the leadership that had carried him within sight of the White House in 1896. However, on imperialism he followed Democratic doctrine as espoused from Jefferson to Cleveland, and by his early objection to imperialism he was more of a molder of public opinion in 1899 than he was in 1896. . . .

Bryan failed to see the incongruity of being on McKinley's side and argued that the treaty was a solemn obligation that must be enforced. He stated that his zeal for his prewar reforms had not abated but that he accepted two new issues—opposition to McKinley's demand for a reorganized army of one hundred thousand men, an issue henceforth called "militarism," and anti-imperialism. McKinley had asked "Who shall haul down the flag that floats over our dead in the Philippines?" Bryan replied:

"The flag is a national emblem and is obedient to the national will. . . . When the American people want it raised, they raise it, when they want it hauled down, they haul it down. . . .

"Shall we keep the Philippines and amend our flag? . . . Shall we add a new star, the blood star, to indicate that we have entered upon a career of conquest? . . . Or shall we adorn our flag with a milky way composed of a multitude of minor stars representing remote and insignificant dependencies?

"No, a thousand times better to haul down the stars and stripes and substitute the flag of an independent republic than to surrender the doctrines that gave glory to 'Old Glory'. . . ."

While Bryan pressed the attack from the stump, Carnegie declared that McKinley's success in getting the treaty ratified depended upon a word from Bryan. But Bryan did not control the Senate in the degree Carnegie suggested. James K. Jones, of Arkansas, the first Democratic senator to break with him over the treaty, told him that the Republicans would accept Democratic help to ratify the treaty and then merely scoff at suggestions that the treaty be nullified by Bryan's proposition of a resolution granting the Filipinos independence.

The third week in January was a critical one, for on January 23 Aguinaldo proclaimed the Philippine Republic and General Otis cabled of an expected rupture. On the twenty-fifth Bacon demanded a vote on his resolution and the Foreign Relations Committee set the date for the vote on the treaty for February 6. Two weeks of executive sessions on the treaty would intervene.

Although apprised of the ugly situation in the Philippines, McKinley clung to the hope that violence would be avoided and that Aguinaldo would not embarrass him while the treaty was in its most critical stage. But Aguinaldo did not want the "large share" in the Philippine government McKinley had promised; he wanted complete independence. McKinley ordered Otis to occupy all strategic points before they fell into Aguinaldo's hands, but Aguinaldo already held them. During the night of February 4 an exchange of shots between sentries of the Nebraska First, ironically, and a Filipino patrol developed into a general engagement in which both American and Filipino lives were lost. According to the administration, the Filipinos had fired first, broken the truce recently established, and thus freed the United States from further obligation. Some believed that Aguinaldo had resorted to hostilities in order to prevent the impending ratification of the treaty, a step supposedly applauded by Bryan and other anti-imperialists. There is no evidence to warrant the latter charge. Proponents of the treaty asserted that the news from Manila made ratification certain, while the anti-imperialists praised American skill and valor but marked the paradox of American soldiers helping to obtain freedom from the Cubans and denying it to the Filipinos. The revolt proved a catalyst; now the wavering senators must make up their minds.

Bryan did not believe that the Filipino attack would affect the outcome of ratification. Those who sought to conquer must expect bloodshed, he said. A resolution promising independence would probably prevent further trouble. Until the nation's policy was determined, however, American soldiers would of course defend American interests.

The vote on the treaty was fifty-seven to twenty-seven, just one more vote than the necessary two thirds. Was Bryan responsible for the ratification of the treaty and for fastening upon the nation the imperialism he so heartily denounced? If so, was he also responsible for the Filipino war? Was he "the most interesting and the least explicit person" in the whole episode; the "baffling figure" who was delivering his party and his country "into the hands of the skillful politicians of expansion and imperialism," and one who "secretly" urged his followers to ratify the treaty? He himself denied that he was responsible for the change of a single vote, flatly contradicting the conclusion of Paxton Hibben that by his influence he "cajoled and dragooned seventeen Democrats and Populists . . . into approving the Spanish treaty." No one knows the exact number of senators Bryan influenced: Carnegie found seven, Julius Pratt fifteen, Hoar seventeen, Garraty "more than a dozen."

On the Saturday before the vote, Lodge counted fifty-eight in favor, with four of these doubtful. Henry Heitfeld (Pop., Idaho) was the first to come over to Lodge, leaving only three doubtfuls, McLaurin, McEnery, and John P. Jones. Half an hour before the opening of the executive session on Monday, February 6, McLaurin came over. McEnery joined up five minutes before roll call, while Jones withheld his vote until after roll call. Thus the proponents of the treaty had their fifty-seven votes.

What about the supposed influence of Bryan with the ten Democrats who voted yea? Morgan and Pettus, of Alabama, Gray and Kenney, of Delaware, and Clay, of Georgia, had announced their support of the treaty by mid-January, when McEnery, McLaurin, and Sullivan were already known as doubt-fuls. Gray thought there was ample time to determine Philippine policy after ratification, although Richard Olney and Hoar sug-gested that some of the fuel Lodge burned in his "engine room" cooking up a federal judgeship for him soon thereafter influenced him. Faulkner, although chairman of the Democratic Congres-sional Campaign Committee in 1894 and 1896, was in high favor with McKinley and voted yea in order to support him. Lindsay was an expansionist; Clay disclaimed Bryan's influence. Sullivan, of Mississippi, sided with Bryan and voted for ratification in order to end the war and proceed with the solution of the Philippine problem.

This leaves McEnery and McLaurin. McEnery apparently was corralled by the persuasive Aldrich and then won over by the promise of the appointment of a federal judge of his choice. Promise of support for his resolution granting Philippine inde-pendence "in due time" undoubtedly influenced him. McLaurin was so changeable in his views and disposition that his integrity, even his rationality, were at times questioned. After speaking against ratification, he suddenly swung to the Republican side. Mrs. McLaurin stated that he was converted on the night before the vote by the news of the Filipino (revolt). He was really won over by the promise of the post office patronage of his state and pledges of support for his resolution calling for the eventual independence of the Philippines.

Of the Populists, Silver Republicans, and the lone Silverite who voted yea, Bryan may have influenced William V. Allen and John P. Jones but not the others—Butler, Harris, Cannon, Teller, Stewart, and Kyle. On the day before the vote, Bryan wired Allen: "Chicago *Chronicle* says you contemplate making speech charging Senators with opposing treaty in order to injure me. Please leave me out of the discussion entirely unless others attack me and then only to defend my right to think and speak as I please like any other citizen." During the morning hours on the sixth, Allen told his colleagues that he did not presume to represent Bryan and that assertions made that he did so were "utterly unfounded, sinister, and false." Pettigrew later wrote a violent disclaimer that Bryan had influenced his vote. Indeed, he maintained that Bryan did not change a single vote. Others have held Bryan almost solely responsible for ratification. According to Hoar, Bryan got all that were needed of his followers to force the treaty through the Senate, making lawful our ownership of the Philippines and, according to high constitutional authorities, making it McKinley's duty to reduce them to submission. That act was a declaration of war against the Filipinos. "And for that war Mr. Bryan is more responsible than any other single person since the treaty left the hands of the President." Hoar credited Bryan with influencing seventeen senators but failed to name them.

Gorman's opposition to ratification stemmed less from conviction than from jealousy of Bryan and hope that the expansion issue would sidetrack the Chicago platform and lead to the presidential nomination for himself. The Democrats and anti-expansionist Republicans had the treaty defeated, he said, until Bryan personally appealed to the Democratic senators. He privately flayed Bryan and demanded that his renomination be prevented, yet he categorically denied that he opposed the treaty for personal political reasons. . . .

Much credit for convincing three of the four doubtfuls goes to Lodge. He wrote Roosevelt that "it was the closest, hardest fight I have ever known," and he modestly gave credit to Aldrich,

Chandler, Hanna, Elkins, Hansbrough, and Carter, not to Bryan. He also complimented Gray for coming out "in a splendid way." "We were down in the engine room and do not get flowers, but we did make the ship move," he told Roosevelt. Aldrich had proved exceedingly active in a desk-to-desk campaign, and the chauvinist Chandler had worked loyally to ratify the treaty. Hanna wrote McKinley on February 7: "In securing the votes of McEnery and McLaurin yesterday I made myself your representative to the extent of a personal plea, so if either should call at the White House today don't fail to express your appreciation of their acts." When Cushman Davis congratulated McKinley on the ratification of the treaty, he said, "When you see Senator Elkins have him tell you about the struggle. I do not believe we could have secured ratification without him." Pettigrew was so outraged by what he saw that he complained to Davis of "the open purchase of votes to ratify this treaty right on the floor of the Senate," including the "purchase" of one Democrat who had remained doubtful until the final session. Lodge also knew of at least one Democrat who was offered a large bribe for a yea vote. Gorman, too, was upset by "the way Hanna and his friends are working this treaty through the Senate. . . . All the railroad influence, which is being worked through Elkins, all the commercial interests and every other interest which can be reached are bringing pressure on Senators in the most shameful way. Some of the things they are doing transcend the bounds of decency." . . .

Much credit for the ratification of the treaty must be given to McKinley. His views were probably unaffected by consideration for the ultimate welfare of the Filipino, but his narrowly partisan administration had created a condition in the Philippines which, even if unpremeditated, certainly influenced various senators. That he saw political expediency in expansionism is readily understandable. Extensive patronage arrangements and promises of good committee assignments were made in his name, and the work of Hanna, Lodge, and Elkins has been recognized as even more effective than that of Bryan. Moreover, resolutions favoring expansion passed by several state legislatures may have helped sway the senators, as did the feeling of popular indignation provoked by the Filipino revolt, for opposition to the President's plan obstructed the Army and was, in a sense, treason. . . .

Had the treaty been rejected, he would have called an extra session in the next twenty-four hours. McKinley thus held the trump card all along, for the new Senate would have lacked seven men who opposed the treaty. "Bryan let his friendliness for McKinley, his desire to do the right and good thing, and his love of peace euchre him into an embarrassing situation," concluded one of Bryan's biographers. According to Merle Curti, "What Mr. Bryan actually did was to crown McKinley's success." . . .

Bryan's tactics with respect to the treaty backfired. Instead of the fast action needed to avoid armed conflict in the Philippines the Republican leaders stalled and threatened to have the treaty go over to the next session. If the treaty had failed, the whole problem would have been thrown back into McKinley's hands or into those of another peace commission. Firm believer in the people's capacity to solve all problems aright, Bryan wanted the people, not the executive, to pass judgment. The Senate passed the treaty but not a resolution stating the nation's purpose to grant the Philippines independence. Caught short, Bryan had no recourse but to submit a *fait accompli* to the people. Despite his making imperialism paramount in 1900, he was defeated.

17   *Thomas A. Bailey*

The 1900 Election Was a Mandate for Partisanship, Not Imperialism

*In an earlier "revisionist" article, Thomas A. Bailey (1902–)
challenged previously held assumptions concerning the role that imperialism had ostensibly played as the dominant issue in the presidential
campaign of 1900. In a succinct, hard-hitting attack on the readiness of
both contemporary analysts and subsequent historians to accept such a
monistic interpretation, Bailey forced a reconsideration of the presidential sweepstakes of that year by citing evidence to demonstrate that
other issues carried much more weight with the ultimate election
power—the individual voter. Thus his closing statement that "one
wonders if these great quadrennial convulsions can ever be a mandate
on anything" becomes even more meaningful if one reflects soberly upon
such subsequent presidential "mandate" elections as those of 1920, 1928,
1940, 1952, 1960 or 1968.*

For a number of years a considerable body of historians has
assumed that imperialism was the "paramount" issue in the campaign of 1900, and that McKinley's triumphant reelection was
a generous endorsement of his policy of expansion. The origins
of this interpretation are not difficult to trace. First of all,
McKinley won by the largest popular plurality that a presidential
candidate had yet polled; and the party in power invariably but
illogically interprets reelection as a blanket endorsement of all
its deeds and misdeeds. Secondly, the Democratic platform stated

SOURCE. Thomas A. Bailey, "Was the Presidential Election of 1900 a
Mandate on Imperialism?," in Alexander DeConde and Armin Rappaport,
eds., *Essays Diplomatic and Undiplomatic of Thomas A. Bailey*, New York:
Appleton-Century-Crofts, Educational Division, Meredith Corporation, 1969,
pp. 141–153; originally published in *Mississippi Valley Historical Review*,
XXIV (June, 1937), pp. 43–52. Reprinted by permission of the Organization
of American Historians and the author.

unequivocally that imperialism was both the "burning" and the "paramount" issue. In his letter of acceptance Bryan stood squarely on this pronouncement, as did his running mate, Adlai E. Stevenson. But unfortunately for the historian the "paramount" issue is not always what the platform and the candidates announce it is going to be.

Seldom has this truth been better illustrated than by the campaign of 1900. Unforeseen economic developments had destroyed the effectiveness of the silver issue; but Bryan, whether through principle or through what he regarded as expediency, forced a free silver plank down the throats of a rebellious Democratic convention. This appears to have been a colossal blunder. It completely ruined whatever chances the Commoner may have had of carrying the gold standard east, particularly in the pivotal empire state. As Thomas B. Reed is reported to have drawled with his characteristic amiability, Bryan "had rather be wrong than president."

The silver plank was a godsend to the harassed Republicans. Driven into a defensive position by the embarrassing Philippine insurrection, they promptly and joyously assumed the offensive with the very weapon that Bryan had thrust into their hands. They could scarcely have asked for anything better than an opportunity to fight the campaign of 1896 over again. McKinley straightway took up the challenge and in his letter of acceptance insisted that currency was the "immediate" issue. The cyclonic Roosevelt, the Republican vice-presidential candidate, echoed these words in his letter of acceptance, and proceeded to rattle the metallic and horrendous skeleton of free silver with unprecedented ferocity. In other words, each party had its own paramount issue, the validity of which the opposition vehemently denied.

It might be argued that because the McKinley ticket won by a plurality of 861,000 votes the sovereign American people decreed that money and not imperialism was the paramount issue. But such an explanation is far too simple to be satisfying. First of all it is undeniable that in any presidential campaign a large percentage of the electorate is not concerned with the issues at all. In the year 1900 several million Republicans and several million Democrats were going to vote the straight party ticket whatever (within reason) the candidates or the issues. But it is a time-honored American custom that parties must have issues. So millions of congenital Democrats worked up what enthusiasm they could over anti-imperialism; and millions of congenital Republicans became alarmed, or attempted to become alarmed, about free silver. The first task is to penetrate this jungle of verbiage and try to determine what issue or issues influenced the votes of those whose minds were open to conviction. In other words, what was the "decisive" issue?

This assignment is by no means a simple one, largely because of the multiplicity and confusion of the issues. Bryan opened the campaign with some heavy blasts about colonialism, imperialism, and militarism; but when he found his audiences singularly unresponsive he swung heavily to trusts, plutocracy, and special privilege. The Republicans emphasized the gold standard, the full dinner pail, continued prosperity, the tariff, patriotism, Bryanistic vagaries, Populism, and class hatred. It would not, in fact, be difficult to make up a list of sixty subjects that were discussed during the campaign, ranging all the way from Crockerism to Pettigrewism and from the St. Louis riots to the Boer War. To add to the confusion ten different parties or political groups actively entered the canvass. . . .

There were many voters who earnestly desired to cast a ballot for both the gold standard and anti-imperialism. But to vote for McKinley and the gold standard was apparently to endorse imperialism; and to vote for Bryan and anti-imperialism was presumably to endorse free silver. Such a militant sound money man as Carl Schurz concluded that imperialism was the more immediate evil, and found himself faced with the "horrible duty" of working for Bryan, or rather against McKinley. On the other hand, ardent anti-imperialists like Andrew Carnegie and Charles Francis Adams regarded economic chaos as the more imminent danger and threw their support to McKinley. It is a significant fact that four of the most effective campaigners for the Republican ticket were leading anti-imperialists: Senators Hoar and Hale, and Representatives Littlefield and McCall.

A large number of Gold Democrats—how many will never be

known—heroically voted for McKinley. They concluded that after the United States had first set its own house in order there would be time enough to turn to the Philippine problem. In post-election statements McKinley, Roosevelt, and Hanna freely acknowledged their indebtedness to Democratic support. In fact, so generally recognized was this defection that the press made repeated references to the non-partisan character of the victory.

A considerable number of those who wished to cast a clear-cut vote against imperialism felt that their only opportunity lay in a third party; but for reasons that need not be discussed here this movement fell through. Others urged Bryan to come out with a ringing pledge not to disturb the gold standard if elected, thus narrowing the paramount issue down to imperialism. But Bryan, foolishly it appears, turned a deaf ear to all such advances. Daniel M. Lord, of the American Anti-Imperialist League, found many anti-imperialists who had decided to vote for McKinley because of their greater fear of free silver; and he suggested to Schurz that a protest signed by several hundred thousand such people before the election would convince McKinley that he had not received a mandate to go ahead with expansion. Schurz replied that this plan would be desirable after the election; but if executed earlier it would merely serve to increase the McKinley vote by enabling the anti-imperialists to salve their consciences. The Springfield *Republican* observed that the suggestion of voting for McKinley first and protesting afterwards won many votes for the Republicans, although, as this journal remarked, the cold figures in no way reflected the voters' "mental reservations." So obviously misleading were the election returns that a number of newspapers called upon McKinley not to interpret the results as an endorsement of imperialism. Indeed, there is some scattered evidence to support the thesis, which obviously can neither be proved nor disproved, that if the question had been placed before the electorate solely on its merits the American people would have voted against retaining the Philippines.

In the minds of many voters the problem was one of choosing the lesser of two evils: the platitudinous and presumably malleable McKinley (T. B. Reed's "Emperor of Expediency") or the heretical and rattle-brained Bryan. "Bryanism and McKinley-ism!" exclaimed Cleveland, "What a choice for a patriotic American!" In the end thousands of voters cast their ballots for McKinley in spite of his Philippine policy—and hoped for the best. They preferred the known weaknesses of McKinley to the wild theories of Bryan. As a Nebraska editor wrote to Cleveland, "It is a choice between evils, and I am going to shut my eyes, hold my nose, vote, go home and disinfect myself." The New York *Nation* suggested for a McKinley banner: "The Nation's Choice—of Evils."

Although it is obvious that any campaign following the colorful crusade of 1896 would seem a tame affair, one is impressed with the fact that there was a marked falling off of the vote in 1900. The general confusion over the issues, combined with a widespread disgust with both of the candidates, caused a considerable number of voters to stay away from the polls. This appears to have been the case with Grover Cleveland, who, according to one newspaper, planned to register his disgust by going duck shooting.

The obvious lack of interest in the campaign was doubtless due in large measure to the fact that the Philippine issue was now more or less stale. The islands had already been under the stars and stripes for over two years; and the American public, leaping with characteristic avidity from one sensation to another, had apparently already begun to classify them among those things settled and accepted. E. V. Abbot noted the "languid interest" in the question of imperialism and observed that "the Republicans weariedly support the administration and the Democrats weariedly oppose it." Moreover the Republicans were confident of victory; and Hanna, dissatisfied with his early efforts to "shake down" the plutocrats, complained that the big enemy of the party was none other than "General Apathy." Finally, in contrast with 1896, the country was busy and prosperous, too fat and contented to be aroused to a high pitch of crusading zeal. . . .

At this point it is possible to answer with some degree of confidence the question as to what was the "decisive" issue in the campaign. Assuming that Bryan had an outside chance to win, the issue that beat him was "Bryanism"—so-called by scores of opposition newspapers. Basically Bryanism was the fear that Bryan would destroy prosperity by overthrowing the gold standard and putting into effect his economic heresies. When the election was over dozens of newspapers insisted that the dread spectre of Bryanism had brought about the result. Even the ebullient Roosevelt wrote with unaccustomed modesty that above McKinley, Hanna, and even himself, "it was Bryan . . . who did most" to bring about the result. That Bryan was a burden to the Democratic cause is further attested by the fact that in general he ran behind his ticket. The "great Commoner" himself admitted, after the election, that the prosperity argument was the most effective one used against him by the Republicans.

One final word about imperialism. If it had been the only issue in the campaign, would the reelection of McKinley have been a clear-cut mandate? The answer still is, no. First of all "imperialism" and "anti-imperialism" were but vague catchwords that meant all things to all men, ranging from a permanent occupation of the Philippines to an immediate and cowardly surrender to Aguinaldo. Bryan certainly did not advocate the latter of these alternatives; but this was the interpretation forced upon him by the opposition, notably Roosevelt, who stormed about the country decrying the dastardly attempt to haul down the flag. Thus imperialism became inextricably identified with patriotism; and a number of voters who wished for ultimate withdrawal supported McKinley because they did not wish to uphold the blood-drenched hands of the enemy. After the election, Bryan himself said that although the prosperity argument was the most potent one used against him, the Republican cry, "Stand by the President" won many votes.

Even if imperialism had been clearly defined and had been the only issue, Bryan's record inspired no great confidence in his willingness to withdraw from the Philippines. Whatever may be said in defense of his rather unexpected course in securing the ratification of the treaty with Spain, it is undeniable that he had begun the campaign on the high note of anti-imperialism and then had shifted to trusts. Such chameleon-like conduct was roundly condemned by the Republicans, including Charles Francis Adams, who remarked in disgust, "I cannot make out whether he is a knave or a fool." And Cleveland wrote, "How do you know what such an acrobat would do on that question (imperialism) if his personal ambition was in the balance?" In other words, many voters concluded, whether correctly or not, that Bryan was just a professional presidential candidate who was only paying lip service to a synthetic issue that might get him into office. The hands were the hands of Esau but the voice was the voice of Bryan.

Even if Bryan had received a clear-cut mandate to withdraw from the Philippines, would his party have permitted him to do so? The recent Spanish conflict, with its fortuitous insular fruits, had in large measure been brought about by Democratic pressure; and although the solid South, for obvious reasons, was going to support Bryan, there was a notoriously strong imperialist sentiment in this section. In addition, the patronage-hungry Democratic party could scarcely have been expected to achieve the self-denial of surrendering these new territories, with their scores of offices for deserving Democrats. Nor did newly developed solicitude of the Democrats for colored peoples ring true to those who knew of conditions in the South. Apparently, as the Republicans taunted their opponents, charity began abroad. Although the Democrats were denouncing imperialism, their platform advocated a protectorate for the Philippines; and was not that imperialism? In fact, a number of observers insisted that the difference between the avowed programs of the two parties was so slight as to amount to a discussion of tweedledum and tweedledee. So it was that many voters, regarding the pronouncements of both Bryan and his party as untrustworthy and insincere, cast their ballots for McKinley because they felt that under his leadership the United States would be able to get out of the Philippines sooner than under that of Bryan.

It seems reasonable to conclude, therefore, that the election of 1900 could not have been an endorsement either of McKinley's leadership in general, or of his policy of expansion. One is even tempted to go a step further and add that because of partisan, personal, sectional, and a host of other domestic considerations, presidential elections have never been and can never be a mandate on any question of foreign policy. Indeed, one wonders if these great quadrennial convulsions can ever be a mandate on anything.

PART FIVE

Epilogue

EPILOGUE

18   *Robin W. Winks*

American and European Imperialism Compared

In the past many Americans have agreed with Richard W. Van Alstyne's observation that "in the United States it is almost a heresy to describe the nation as an empire." But the participatory involvement of America in global politics in the years since World War II has forced many Americans to reconsider their national past, in terms of the motivation underlying America's fin-de-siècle overseas expansion. The necessity of viewing American actions from a non-American perspective was the inspiration for a series of broadcasts over the Voice Of America, of which this essay by Robin W. Winks (1930–   ) was one. Educated at Colorado and Johns Hopkins (Ph.D., 1957) he is currently teaching Commonwealth history at Yale. Utilizing a conceptual approach, Winks has tried to compare the imperial institutions of the United States (such as they were—or are) with those of its European counterparts, while at the same time posing questions for further study. Do you agree with his a priori assumption that "imperialism was a practice; colonialism a state of mind"? Does Winks regard American continental expansion as a form of imperialism? Finally, what is his judgment on the use—or misuse—of American power in promoting its expansionist aims, and what does this portend for the future?

Many Americans have assumed that there was no period of American imperialism. Others admit to a brief imperialist past

SOURCE. Robin W. Winks, "Imperialism," from Chapter 18 of *The Comparative Approach to American History* edited by C. Vann Woodward. Copyright 1968 by C. Vann Woodward, Basic Books, Inc., Publishers, New York. Reprinted by permission.

but prefer to clothe that past in other words. We were an expansionist nation, some historians argue, but not an imperialist one, a distinction more Jesuitical than useful. Yet other apologists suggest that since American growth was the direct result of a unique American sense of mission, of a Messianic impulse to set the world right which, even if wrongheaded, was sincere, humanitarian, progressive, and in general benevolent, the United States was apart from and above the ventures of the European scramblers for colonies. But most imperialisms have been rooted in a sense of mission, and the American sense differs from that of other nations chiefly in that the United States emphasized different characteristics. The British sense of mission sprang from a conviction of cultural superiority, the Japanese from a racial message thinly veiled in paternal rhetoric, the German from an impulse toward a preordained dialectic, and the Communist sense of mission from what was conceived to be a sure knowledge of the world's ultimate needs and ends. And to say that we all are sinners does not remove the necessity to see whether and how our sins have differed.

Imperialism was not always in ill-repute, of course. In Britain in the 1880's and 1890's, Chamberlain and Rosebery were proud to call themselves imperialists. They were helping unfortunate peoples around the world to come into the light; they were lifting Britain, and not at the expense of nonwhites but at the expense of other, highly competitive European powers. Whatever befell the subjects of imperial control was, on the whole, to their good. An advanced radical such as Charles Dilke and a conservative such as J. A. Froude could agree upon the righteousness of as well as on the need for imperial expansion; and while liberals and conservatives placed different orders of priority upon their respective rationales, they also agreed upon the basic mix: Britain must reform itself at home and make itself fit for an imperial role while expanding abroad in order to extend to the unenlightened the many benefits of a rationalized, ordered society. Improved sanitation and education, the equal administration of the law and the equal application of justice, the stamping out of slavery, debt bondage, suttee, polygamy, nakedness, and bride price—all seemed legitimate goals when viewed from within the liberal framework of the time. Theodore Roosevelt, too, thought that the vigorous Anglo-Saxon should carry forth the torch of progress; and, not unlike that hoary old radical and voice of the people, Walt Whitman, he wanted a race of splendid mothers. . . .

Imperialism was a practice; colonialism was a state of mind. Whether a powerful nation extended its control, its influence, or merely its advice over another people, those so controlled or so advised not unnaturally resented the controller. Indeed, we have all been colonies mentally at one time or another; no one likes, as they say, to be over a barrel. Much indignity lies in any subservient position, and yet there will always be the powerful and the powerless, and the people with the most power may not escape being the nation that is powerless, as Britain learned at Suez and as the United States is learning today. There is obvious indignity in never being the mover but always the moved, in waiting to see how a foreign capital or a foreign embassy will decide one's fate.

Behind the practice we call imperialism lay many strands of thought which were drawn together near the end of the nineteenth century to provide a rationale for expansive policies. The natural science, like the social organization of the time, emphasized selectivity, categories, hierarchies. There were natural orders of being, as there were natural orders of animal life, and nothing was more natural to political man than to assume that, as Walter Bagehot wrote, there were parallels between physics and politics. The new science taught "objectivity" and in the nineteenth century objectivity meant measurement, not cultural relativism but the opposite, the desire to place races, peoples, and cultures into classifiable categories. Cranial capacity, the length and width of heads, body odor, the color of the skin and the nature of the hair, all were measured, charted, and used to conclude that fundamental differences separated people. The vulgarization of the theories of Charles Darwin was combined with the romanticist's penchant for finding decadence wherever he looked, and the combination justified seeing the world as a jungle in which only the fittest might survive. The opening sentence of Count Arthur de Gobineau's *Essai sur l'Inégalité des Races Humaines,* published in 1853, spoke for the new pessimism that was, in fact, romantic: "The fall of civilization is the most striking and, at the same time, the most obscure of all phenomena of history." This pessimism was to run on through Spengler, through Toynbee, to the present. Arnold Toynbee was to write of the "natural dysgenic effects" that occur in societies; he was to find some groups—the Polynesians and the Jews, for example— suspended on plateaus where insufficient responses to overwhelming challenges had left them. The best men could hope to do was to turn back animality, or animality would take over the world. And to these strands of romance and science were added yet others—the Christian desire to save, to convert, and to enlighten, the commercial impulse to markets, the geopolitical and military notion of strategic values, the desire for adventure, the national thrust to a place in the sun, the national need for *la gloire....*

The United States was part of this climate of opinion. American responses to some of the assumptions of European imperialists were bound to be negative, for the United States had grown, after all, out of a former colonial empire. The assumptions that Americans made about imperial responsibility were conditioned by an awareness of distance from the scenes of European conflicts, by a knowledge that the American people were an amalgam of many of the peoples of the world, some themselves representative of the victims of imperial struggles, and from an emotional predisposition to apply the basic tenets of republicanism to the imperial situation.

Perhaps here lies the most significant differences between the American empire and other imperial growths of a comparable time. Most Americans, including their overseas administrators, hoped to make the colonial societies over in the American model so that they could qualify for self-government or for admission into the Union itself. This assumption produced, as Whitney T. Perkins has pointed out, "a safety valve of sorts in an inherent bias toward the extension of self-government." This bias was more far-reaching than the British bias toward establishing representative institutions on the Westminster model, for it was there from the beginning, and republican principles were maintained for the so-called subject peoples as well as for the dominant nation. The territories acquired from Mexico whether by conquest or by purchase, became states of the Republic. So too did Alaska and Hawaii; and although the time needed to complete the necessary transformation before statehood became a reality was a long one, the assumption always was present that independence or statehood was the goal. The safety valve thus prevented the buildup within the colonies of a long-term ruling elite imposed from outside. It also decreased the intensity of local nationalist movements. While the British moved slowly toward their concept of indirect rule in East Africa, of governing through the already existing tribal structures, the United States applied a form of indirect rule almost immediately, and especially so in the Philippines, in Puerto Rico, and in Samoa. While the British anticipated that the Indians one day would be an independent people, as late as 1930 otherwise farsighted British spokesmen could suggest that such a day would not come for another century. Impatient, as usual, Americans presumed that their imperial role would be a short one, as indeed it was.

Unwilling to admit that dependency was more than a passing phase, American leaders were slow to think through the implications of having an empire. No permanent overseas civil service or military establishment, no educational system meant primarily to provide a continuing imperial tradition, arose to perpetuate imperial dogma. It is not without significance that American romantic novelists of empire, such as Richard Harding Davis, men of the same cloth as G. A. Henty, H. Rider Haggard, John Buchan, and Rudyard Kipling, wrote primarily of empires the United States did not hold, seldom using American colonial locales for their adventures. Perhaps the clearest proof that Americans assumed that their empire would be more transient than most may be seen in the fact that there was no Colonial Office, no Ministère des Colonies. The various territories were allocated to the Department of State, of the Interior, the Navy, and War; and when, in 1934, a Division of Territories and Island Possessions was created within the Department of the Interior, Guam and Samoa nonetheless were left to the Navy and the Panama Canal Zone to the Army.

The question is not, therefore, whether the United States or any other nation used power; rather, the questions are, how was this power first mobilized against the less powerful, and how was it ultimately employed? And in the answers to these two questions we may find some areas of contrast between American and, as an example, British imperial experiences.

The facts are clear enough. Most observers would agree in identifying two major periods of American expansion before 1939. The first of these, from perhaps 1803 until 1853, was a period of internal growth, of movement across the land from the eastern seaboard to the west coast, and of two wars—that of 1812–1814 with Britain and the Mexican War of 1846–1848—which, while not primarily concerned with the acquisition of new territory, nonetheless involved considerable and admitted expansionist interests. When in 1853 the United States purchased an additional corner of land from Mexico for ten million dollars, expansion within contiguous areas was complete.

Was this first period of expansion imperialistic? Perhaps. Certainly the rhetoric that accompanied it was so, and some of the same genuinely held and humanitarian if arrogant views were present in 1812 and in 1846 as sustained the British, for example, during their forward movement in Southeast Asia and Africa after 1870. In 1859 a Congressman from Mississippi envisioned the incorporation of the whole of Mexico, Central America, South America, Cuba, and the West Indies into the Republic, just as Cecil Rhodes later wished to see the entirety of at least the eastern sweep of the African continent painted red on the imperial maps. If the same Congressman also suggested that France and England might be annexed as well, while permitting them to retain their local legislatures for the regulation of local affairs, his hyperbole can be matched by much that Thomas Carlyle, Charles Kingsley, Sir Charles Dilke, or Lord Lugard wrote or said about various African kingdoms and reasonably viable Indian states.

Certainly the roots of the later period of American expansion overseas lie in the pre-Civil War past, for it was then that the American idea of a national mission developed. The secularization of the earlier Puritan concepts, the growing sense of the covenant the American people had made with themselves during the Revolution and within their Constitution, and the heightened awareness of and belief in a unique American destiny, led many Americans sincerely to support any of several arguments for expansion. Many believed they were liberating Canadians from British despotism in 1814 and freeing Mexicans from harsh and undemocratic rule in 1847. The doctrine of natural right, the European idea of natural boundaries to which a nation or a people naturally must expand, the desire to extend the "area of freedom" to those less fortunate, the thought that energetic, egalitarian Americans could better use the soil, even that they might regenerate people who too long had lived under effete and declining European institutions, including European churches— all these impulses toward reform lay behind the expansion of the pre-Civil War years.

Because the United States had a continent to conquer, it developed its first empire internally, incorporating territory into the body politic in a way that European nations having to seek overseas outlets for their energies, their people, their goods, their investments, and their doctrines, could neither understand nor attempt. If Britain's third empire lay in Africa, America's first empire lay at hand, merely across the wide Missouri. An imperial democracy might grow within the continent. Thus continentalism, not imperialism, occupied the driving American energies until near the end of the century. As Frederick Jackson Turner was to point out in his essay on the significance of sections in American history, the South and the West at differing times were to think of themselves as colonies of the North and the East. The South was, after all, a conquered territory under military occupation between 1865 and 1877; and the West was, in its eyes and often in the eyes of Wall Street as well, a subject land. Further, Americans did not need coolies or castes in order to create an American *raj*. There always was the Negro to stand at the bottom of the social and economic scale, and there were the Indians to be pressed onto reservations.

The idea of mission was reinforced by the Federal victory in the Civil War. In 1867 the United States purchased Alaska from Russia. Following a period of internal concern for reconstructing Southern state governments, for reshaping the machinery of business, and for general domestic economic and social growth, Americans turned outward. The second major period of American expansion, and the first to propel America overseas, coincided with the world-wide wave of imperial annexations associated with the British, French, and German empires and with the awakening of Japan. If the earlier period were merely expansionist, as some contend, the growth between 1898 and 1920 was genuinely imperialist. . . .

However administered, three differences stand out between the American and other empires. Most British acquisitions between 1870 and 1920 were for the purpose of stabilizing already held possessions, arising from turbulent frontiers lying across some unoccupied and intermediate hinterland, turbulence that created vacuums into which the British feared other nations would rush. American annexations, largely consisting of islands, shared the strategic and preventive aspects of European imperialism, but in terms of scale alone the American holdings were relatively insignificant, and each acquisition did not to nearly the same extent create an ever-widening circle of new conflicts. Second, there was no grand design to American expansionism, no overall world strategy, no forward movement as in British Malaya, tied either to a containment policy, as Britain's island acquisitions were in part, or tied to an assumption of semi-permanence. The American occupations of both Haiti and the Dominican Republic were short-lived, seen from the outset to be temporary, with limited objectives in mind. This makes the occupations no less imperialistic, of course, but it does illustrate the makeshift nature of the American empire.

Most important, perhaps, is the by no means complimentary fact that the American imperialism was more culturally insidious than that of Britain or Germany, although perhaps not more so than that of France. To qualify for self-government among American states, colonial dependencies had to be utterly transformed, and the Americans often showed very little respect for Spanish culture in Puerto Rico, for Samoan life in Tutuila, or for the structure of the old Hawaiian kingdom. The French, with their *mission civilisatrice*, were equally willing to insist that, to be civilized, the colonized must learn the language and customs of the conqueror. The British, ever more pragmatic, were content to administer through an elite, creating classes of Anglo-Indians and other cultural hyphenates but leaving the fundamental nature of the indigenous culture unchanged. Since they never anticipated the day when India would become part of the United Kingdom, and not until the 1920's did responsible officials give serious thought even to the loose linkage now involved in Commonwealth ties, wholesale Anglicizing was unnecessary. Precisely because the Americans did anticipate rapid progress toward assimilation did they insist upon such brutally fast Americanization.

As a British historian of empire, David K. Fieldhouse, has pointed out, what set the American empire apart, then, was the attempt to fit colonial possessions into the Procrustian bed of republicanism. No one provided a theoretical base for permanent colonialism, for the new territories were to be ushered into the United States on the basis of the same machinery, already established by the Constitution, that was used for Kentucky and Tennessee in the 1790's, for Colorado in 1876, and for Arizona in 1912. Congress extended full citizenship to the dependencies —to Puerto Ricans in 1917, to the Virgin Islands in 1927, to Guamanians in 1950. Representative government came quickly, responsible government slowly, and Congress exercised over the legislative bodies within the colonies the same kind of ultimate veto that lay in Britain's Colonial Laws Validity Act of 1865.

A difference of considerable importance lay in the fact that the American empire was the only one, other than the Russian, which formed a single economic system. Alaska and Hawaii were brought under the American tariff upon annexation, Puerto Rico in 1900, and the Philippine Islands in 1909. The advantages of such a system accrued almost entirely to the colonies, for all were primary producers who would have found their chief markets in the United States in any event. That the colonies felt more economically benefited than exploited may be seen from the Philippines' rejection of an offer of independence in 1933 because it meant gradual exclusion from the American protective system. Nor did the United States gain economically from the colonies. In 1925, a high point, only 4.9 per cent of

American exports went to any of the colonial areas, including those Caribbean states bound to the United States by treaty. Nor did the colonies become important for capital—by World War II, Puerto Rico and the Philippines together held only 2.5 per cent of total overseas American investment, a figure ridiculously tiny compared to the sums placed in independent nations such as Mexico and Canada.

Perhaps here we discover a large area of comparability between American and European imperialisms. France, still primarily concerned with agricultural problems, stands apart from many generalizations, but Britain assuredly also realized little direct economic gain from her colonies. The British also preferred to place investment capital in areas that need not be annexed. The British informal empire, an empire of trade, investment, and influence, extended into the Middle East, to Argentina, and to the Baltic states, just as an American informal empire existed in Latin America, in Canada, and in parts of China. But such nations also gained from such contacts, as any study of the growth of the Canadian industry or of Argentine rails would show. Informal empires were a mixed blessing, but mixed they were, doctrinaire ideologies notwithstanding.

The American empire may be contrasted to those of the European powers in another way, however. The United States had grown out of an earlier empire, and having fought a revolutionary war to gain its independence of Britain, it continued to hold to certain principles which, as we have seen, injected republican assumptions into colonial relationships. Further, all of the colonial possessions acquired by the United States, with the exception of Hawaii, had belonged to another nation before. They were not formerly independent states, they had not experienced a recent period of local autonomy, as Natal did under the Boers, as the Indian princely states had done before the British East India Company arrived upon the scene, or as the Malay States did under their sultans. Cuba, Puerto Rico, the Philippines, and Guam had been under Spanish control, the Virgin Islands under Danish, Alaska under Russian, Samoa under German and British, and the Canal Zone under Colombian. Former concepts of independence were not silenced and, in some cases, were introduced for the first time. The American imperial acquisitions might thus be best compared to those areas added to the British Empire at the Treaty of Versailles, as the spoils of war, not the spoils of trade. In effect, the American empire was not unlike the new colonial holdings of Australia and New Zealand—a ricochet empire, picked up as the by-product of other events, and ironically acquired by nations which themselves had grown out of former dependency status. . . .

What, then, have we said of American imperialism? That, like all imperialisms, it was contradictory and that it could make an entire people appear to be hypocritical. When Woodrow Wilson set out to make the world safe for democracy, he spoke for *Realpolitik* as well as for humanitarianism, for the kind of democracy for which he wished to make the world safe was American democracy. But if he thought that he must teach South Americans to elect good men, he also remembered himself sufficiently not to do so. "We can afford," he thought, "to exercise the self-restraint of a really great nation which realizes its own strength and scorns to misuse it."

We have also said that similarities in motivation do not prove similarities in execution. The imperial experience, whether viewed from the gunboats of the expanding powers or from the beaches of the colonized peoples, must involve more than the first part of the story. Because the United States had no established church, no class of permanent civil servants, no entrenched system of private and privileged education, and no well-established military tradition, the American imperial movement was reinforced by fewer institutions. While G. A. Henty rode *Through the Khyber Pass* and Henri Fauconnier sought out *The Soul of Malaya*, American novelists did not write of Samoa, Guam, or Puerto Rico. Racism, romanticism, pseudo-science, and Christianity worked in roughly similar ways in British and American societies but they were projected into the colonies somewhat differently.

There are, perhaps, four questions which one might pose of any imperial relationship. What was the nature of the white settlers sent into the new country? What was the nature of the indigenous people? What was the degree of commitment on the part of the metropolitan power to retention of the territory and for what purposes? Within what geographical compass would the drama be played out? Since the United States sent few settlers into its empire, and since the areas, with the exception of the Philippines and Alaska, were quite small, the American answer to the first and last of these questions usually differed from the British, French, or Russian response. There rise the differences. In the answers to the second and third of the questions rise the similarities. One does not wish to reduce a complex problem to futile simplicities, but nonetheless one suspects that the American imperial experience is comparable to that of other nations only briefly, somewhat incidentally, and then but half the time.

BIBLIOGRAPHICAL ESSAY

Any serious study of the history of American overseas expansion must rest, in the final analysis, on the utilization of primary source materials. There is a virtual plethora of manuscript sources available in various locations in the United States, but they are very uneven in content and quality. For example, one can learn much more about the evolution of foreign policy decisions by the McKinley Administration during the Spanish-American War by examining the papers of John Bassett Moore, Assistant Secretary of State at that time, than one can by the most careful scrutiny of the papers of President McKinley or Secretary of State William R. Day. Most of the important personal collections for the period are on deposit in the Manuscripts Division of the Library of Congress. The student should have recourse to Philip M. Hamer (ed.), *A Guide to Archives and Manuscripts in the United States* (rev. ed., New Haven, 1965), for the location of other important manuscript collections on deposit in library and archival collections in the United States.

The National Archives in Washington, D.C., are the principal source of documentary evidence for those interested in a fuller understanding of the diplomatic and military activity of the period. Of particular importance are the collections of diplomatic correspondence, arranged in decimal file, between Washington and its overseas outposts, which can be found in Record Group No. 59. For a better appreciation of the policy roles of various cabinet departments and Congressional committees during this period, one should also consult, among others, Record Groups No. 38 (Office of Naval Intelligence), No. 45 (Office of Naval Records and Library), No. 107 (Office of the Secretary of War), No. 165 (Office of the Chief of Staff), and No. 225 (Joint Army and Navy Board). A useful aid for scanning European archival collections relevant to American foreign policy is Daniel H. Thomas and Lynn M. Case (eds.), *Guide to the Diplomatic Archives of Western Europe* (Philadelphia, 1959).

Among the rich collection of printed sources available on the subject, the reader's attention is directed immediately to the annual
publications of the State Department, *Papers Relating to the Foreign
Relations of the United States, 1861–* (Washington, 1862–). As a
general rule, the State Department usually released the pertinent
documents for publication within the calendar year in which the
events had transpired. However, the events of 1898 were deemed so
controversial that the pertinent documents for that year were not
published until 1901, after McKinley had been safely re-elected. In
the years since World War II the State Department has fallen even
further behind in the publication of these annual volumes (they are
about twenty-five years in arrears at the present time), but they are
still decades ahead of their major European counterparts in their
willingness to make such information available to interested scholars.

The domestic counterpart of the *Foreign Relations Papers* is the
U.S. *Congressional Record* (Washington, 1874–), which is a valuable
barometer of legislative and popular feelings on various issues at any
given time. A necessary complement for the study of foreign policy is
the *Journal of the Executive Proceedings of the Senate of the United
States of America,* published individually for each two-year session of
the Congress. A partial *Journal* of the executive sessions of the 55th
Congress (March, 1897 to March, 1899) was published in 1909, but
the veil of secrecy concerning three such executive sessions of the
Senate in April and May of 1898 was only removed on 28 January
1969, as a result of a special resolution introduced by Senator Edward
M. Kennedy (D-Mass.). The transcript of these proceedings can be
found in Record Group No. 46 at the National Archives. Four other
valuable printed government sources for obtaining a better understanding of the events of 1898 are U.S. Senate, 55th Congress, 2nd
Session, Doc. No. 681, *Annexation of Hawaii* (Washington, 1898);
Ministerio de Estado, *Spanish Diplomatic Correspondence and Docu-
ments, 1896–1900* (translation, Washington, 1905); U.S. Senate, 55th
Congress, 3rd Session, Doc. No. 62, *A Treaty of Peace Between the
United States and Spain* (Washington, 1899), which contains the
formal protocols presented by both sides at the Paris peace negotiations,
as well as the testimony of the American witnesses there; and U.S.
Senate, 56th Congress, 1st Session, Doc. No. 221, *U.S. Commission
Appointed by the President to Investigate the Conduct of the War
Department in the War with Spain* (8 vols., Washington, 1900). The
last named is perhaps better known as the *Dodge Commission Report.*

No student of the period should overlook the newspapers and

periodicals of that time. Despite the adverse publicity concerning the antics of Hearst and Pulitzer, the press, in general, was undergoing a distinct change for the better, because of new technical advances, improved methods of news gathering (especially among the wire services), and, most important, higher standards for editing and news analysis. Thus papers like the New York *Times,* the New York *Tribune,* the *Washington Post,* the *Chicago Tribune,* and the Springfield *Republican* were, for the most part, valid sources of contemporary history, as were business journals such as the *Wall Street Journal* and the New York *Journal of Commerce and Commercial Bulletin.* Among the more important periodicals of the period were *Bradstreet's, The Century Magazine, Forum, The Independent, Iron Age, Journal of the American Asiatic Association, The Nation, North American Review, Outlook,* and *Review of Reviews.*

Finally, the unpublished Ph.D. dissertations and M.A. theses written on various topics pertaining to the period are a valuable source of information. Two useful guides to tracking them down are Warren F. Kuehl (ed.), *Dissertations in History: An Index to Dissertations Completed in History Departments of United States and Canadian Universities, 1873–1960* (Lexington, 1965); and the triennial publication of the American Historical Association, *List of Doctoral Dissertations in History in Progress or Completed at Colleges and Universities in the United States Since* (1958, 1961, 1964, 1967, and so on).

The volume of secondary literature available on the topic is staggering; one could write an independent volume just listing the applicable titles but, for reasons of space, only those that seem most pertinent or provocative will be cited here. The most disconcerting tendency on the part of too many writers on American expansion in the nineteenth century is their propensity for regarding America as the *alpha* and *omega* of international relations, rather than trying to place the role of the United States in a world setting and context. Though somewhat dated in its research, the most useful introduction in this respect is William L. Langer, *The Diplomacy of Imperialism* (2nd ed., New York, 1965). Other important studies contributing to a better conceptual understanding of imperialism as an international, institutional life-style in the nineteenth century are David K. Fieldhouse, *The Colonial Empires: A Comparative Survey* (London, 1966); Richard Koebner, *Empire* (Cambridge, England, 1961); Richard Koebner and H. D. Schmidt, *Imperialism: The Story and Significance of a Political Word, 1840–1960* (Cambridge, England, 1963); John Gallagher, Ronald Robinson and Alice Denny, *Africa and the Victorians: The Official*

Mind of Imperialism (New York, 1961) ; and A. P. Thornton, *Doctrines of Imperialism* (New York, 1965). Older, but still valuable, ideological critiques on the subject include John A. Hobson, *Imperialism* (new ed., Ann Arbor, 1965) ; V. I. Lenin, *Imperialism: The Highest Stage of Capitalism* (rev. 2nd ed., New York, 1934) ; Joseph A. Schumpeter, *Imperialism and Social Classes* (New York, 1951) ; and Raymond Aron, *Peace and War, a Theory of International Relations* (New York, 1966). A valuable collection of essays on comparative imperial systems is George H. Nadel and Perry Curtis (eds.), *Imperialism and Colonialism* (New York, 1964).

In recent years two American scholars have attempted to interpret American overseas expansion at the turn of the century in a less parochial context. In *Denial of Empire: The United States and Its Dependencies* (Leyden, 1962), Whitney T. Perkins has essayed a number of comparisons with the imperial systems employed by the European powers at that time. Ernest R. May, in *Imperial Democracy: The Emergence of America as a Great Power* (New York, 1961), employed a multiarchival analysis of the interaction between the European governments and the United States in introducing the latter country into the family of world powers in the years 1895–1899. His conclusion that, before 1895, the United States was a nonentity in world power politics and that, by the end of the century, it "had greatness thrust upon it" seems unwarranted by the facts prior to 1895. The most succinct conflicting view in this respect is Thomas A. Bailey, "America's Emergence as a World Power: The Myth and the Verity," *Pacific Historical Review*, XXX (February, 1961), pp. 1–16. Moreover, May's work is marred by a dim, ambivalent perception of the domestic forces operating upon the decision-making processes in the Cleveland and McKinley administrations. He seems much too willing to accept outdated stereotypes of these two presidents. In a sequel volume, *American Imperialism: A Speculative Essay* (New York, 1968), May attempted to analyze the domestic forces that motivated the movement toward American imperialism. Rather than place the blame on indigenous American forces, May ascribed its inspiration to European publicists who confused and led astray elitist American "opinion leaders" who, in turn, persuaded their fellow countrymen, both in and out of power, to embark upon a program of overseas acquisitions. The documentation available tends to refute such a thesis; at best the book can be regarded as little more than its subtitle states—a speculative essay.

Among those scholars who have attempted to analyze American expansion as a historical continuum, the two most stimulating and

provocative are Richard W. Van Alstyne and William A. Williams. In
The Rising American Empire (New York, 1960), Van Alstyne stressed
the conceptual continuity of American continental and overseas ex-
pansion from the Revolution to the era of Woodrow Wilson. A strong
counter argument to this thesis is presented by Frederick Merk in
Manifest Destiny and Mission in American History (New York, 1963).
Less forceful, but similar, analyses of the Merk position are Albert K.
Weinberg, *Manifest Destiny: A Study of Nationalist Expansionism in
American History* (Baltimore, 1935); Edward M. Burns, *The American
Idea of Mission: Concepts of National Purpose and Identity* (New
Brunswick, 1957); and Arthur A. Ekirch, Jr., *Ideas, Ideals, and Ameri-
can Diplomacy: A History of Their Growth and Interaction* (New
York, 1966). Though more limited in subject treatment, the follow-
ing are valuable supplements to Van Alstyne's ideas on continentalism:
Henry Nash Smith, *Virgin Land* (Cambridge, 1950); D. F. Warner,
*The Idea of Continental Union: Agitation for the Annexation of
Canada to the United States, 1849–1893* (Lexington, 1960); and the
brilliant study of Ralph H. Gabriel, *The Course of American Demo-
cratic Thought* (2nd ed., New York, 1956). Charles Vevier has also
made an important contribution in "American Continentalism: An
Idea Of Expansion, 1845–1910," *American Historical Review*, LXV
(January, 1960), pp. 323–335.

William A. Williams was no doubt influenced by Charles A. Beard's
The Idea of National Interest (New York, 1934) and Fred H. Harrington's *God, Mammon and the Japanese* (Madison, 1944) in the writing
of his three most important works to date; viz., *The Contours of American History* (Cleveland, 1961), *The Tragedy of American Diplomacy*
(rev. ed., New York, 1962), and *The Great Evasion* (Chicago, 1964).
In each, Williams continues the development of his central thesis that,
obsessed by the desire for overseas markets, the United States chose
"informal empire" at the expense of an opportunity to construct a
cooperative integrated society at home. This unduly involved the
country in international power politics and provided the setting for
domestic social and economic chaos. Williams' ideas concerning the
prevalence of a conscious *a priori* economic policy on the part of successive Presidential administrations, regardless of party affiliation, has
been more fully developed for this period by three of his former students; Walter LaFeber, *The New Empire: An Interpretation of American Expansion, 1860–1898* (Ithaca, 1963); Thomas J. McCormick,
China Market: America's Quest for Informal Empire, 1893–1901 (Chicago, 1967); and Lloyd C. Gardner (ed.), *A Different Frontier* (Chi-

cago, 1966). Whether this interpretation will become the dominant one in the years ahead is still a moot question. The attack has already been mounted against the so-called "Wisconsin School" *et opera omnia*. The most abrasive of these assaults thus far is John Braeman's "The Wisconsin School Of American Diplomatic History: A Critique" (an unpublished paper delivered at the annual meeting of the Organization of American Historians on 27 April 1967). Irwin Unger has presented a more balanced view of the "Wisconsin School" in "The 'New Left' and American History: Some Recent Trends in United States Historiography," *American Historical Review*, LXXII (July, 1967), pp. 1237–1263.

Two of the most valuable background studies for the period under discussion are David M. Pletcher, *The Awkward Years: American Foreign Relations Under Garfield and Arthur* (Columbia, Mo., 1962), and J. A. S. Grenville and George B. Young, *Politics, Strategy and American Diplomacy: Studies in Foreign Policy, 1873–1917* (New Haven, 1966). The former is the single best work to date on the decade of the 1880's and has important implications for a proper understanding of the more publicized events of the following decade. The work by Grenville and Young is actually a series of eleven essays that emphasize the working interrelationship between diplomatic policy and military strategy. The authors explode a few myths in the process, such as the inflated importance of Alfred Thayer Mahan (Admiral Stephen B. Luce, his patron, was a much more historically significant figure); the over-publicized role of the "large policy" clique headed by Lodge, Theodore Roosevelt and Mahan; and the supposed "constructive pacifism" of Grover Cleveland. Further background information on the activities of the War and Navy Department during this period can be found in Leonard D. White, *The Republican Era: 1869–1901* (New York, 1958), an administrative history of the period; Russell F. Weigley, *Towards an American Army* (New York, 1962); Stephen E. Ambrose, *Upton and the Army* (Baton Rouge, 1964); Robert Seager II, "Ten Years Before Mahan: The Unofficial Case For The New Navy, 1880–1890," *Mississippi Valley Historical Review*, XL (December, 1953), pp. 491–512; Walter R. Herrick, Jr., *The American Naval Revolution* (Baton Rouge, 1966); and William R. Braisted, *The United States Navy in the Pacific, 1897–1909* (Austin, 1958), a work of prime importance. The best analysis of Mahan's thinking is still William E. Livezey, *Mahan on Sea Power* (Norman, Okla., 1947), but one should nevertheless read the first chapter of Mahan's seminal work, *The Influence of Sea Power Upon History* (Boston, 1890).

Important regional background studies that examine issues in the Caribbean area are: Samuel Flagg Bemis, *The Latin-American Policy of the United States* (New York, 1943); Dexter Perkins, *The Monroe Doctrine, 1867–1907* (Baltimore, 1937); Rayford Logan, *The Diplomatic Relations of the United States with Haiti, 1776–1891* (Chapel Hill, 1941); the two works by Charles C. Tansill, *The Purchase of the Danish West Indies* (Baltimore, 1932) and *The United States and Santo Domingo, 1798–1873* (Baltimore, 1938); and Lester D. Langley, *The Cuban Policy of the United States* (New York, 1968). The Marxist-oriented study of Philip S. Foner, *The History of Cuba and Its Relations with the United States* (2 vols. to date, New York, 1962–   ), should be used with caution. For the Far East, consult the still-useful Tyler Dennett, *Americans in Eastern Asia: A Critical Study of United States Policy in the Far East in the Nineteenth Century* (New York, 1922), as well as William L. Neumann, *America Encounters Japan: From Perry To MacArthur* (Baltimore, 1963). Akira Iriye, a Japanese-born, American-educated scholar with a mastery of Chinese sources has written a superb synthesis of American relations with East Asia in *Across the Pacific* (New York, 1967). For German-American problems in the Pacific see Alfred Vagts, *Deutschland und die Vereinigten Staaten in der Weltpolitik* (2 vols., New York, 1935). Edward H. Zabriskie has surveyed the problems with Tsarist Russia in *American-Russian Rivalry in the Far East: A Study in Diplomacy and Power Politics, 1895–1914* (Philadelphia, 1946).

Most of the general domestic histories of the period have not kept abreast of the latest scholarship in the field, but the following are useful for their treatment of party politics, social and economic developments. The best of recent general syntheses on the period are John A. Garraty, *The New Commonwealth, 1877–1890* (New York, 1968); Harold U. Faulkner, *Politics, Reform and Expansion, 1890–1900,* (New York, 1959); Samuel P. Hays, *The Response to Industrialism, 1885–1914* (Chicago, 1957); and Robert H. Wiebe, *The Search for Order, 1877–1920* (New York, 1967). Ray Ginger's *Age of Excess: The United States from 1877 to 1914* (New York, 1965), is the most provocative and uneven of the group; its acerbic bibliographical essay is often better reading than the text.

Matthew Josephson's two muckraking studies on the politics of the period, *The Politicos, 1865–1896* (New York, 1938), and *The President Makers, 1896–1912* (New York, 1940), have been balanced by the more recent efforts of J. Rogers Hollingsworth, *The Whirligig of Politics: The Democracy of Cleveland and Bryan* (Chicago, 1963);

David J. Rothman, *Politics and Power: The United States Senate, 1869–1901* (Cambridge, 1966), and H. Wayne Morgan, *From Hayes to McKinley: National Party Politics, 1877–1896* (Syracuse, 1969). For an examination of socioeconomic developments during the period, the best surveys are Edward C. Kirkland, *Industry Comes of Age, 1860–1897* (New York, 1961); Harold U. Faulkner, *The Decline of Laissez-Faire, 1897–1917* (New York, 1951); Fred A. Shannon, *The Farmer's Last Frontier: Agriculture, 1860–1897* (New York, 1945); Richard Hofstadter, *The Age of Reform* (New York, 1955); and Norman Pollack's aggressive *The Populist Response to Industrial America* (Cambridge, 1962). An important unpublished study is Tom E. Terrill, "The Tariff And American Foreign Policy, 1880–1892" (Ph.D. dissertation, University of Wisconsin, 1966).

For varying degrees of coverage and quality on the intellectual currents of the period, in addition to those cited above, see Richard Hofstadter, *Social Darwinism in American Thought* (Philadelphia, 1944); Morton G. White, *Social Thought in America: The Revolt Against Formalism* (New York, 1949); Henry S. Commager, *The American Mind* (New Haven, 1950); and Eric F. Goldman, *Rendezvous with Destiny* (New York, 1952). Still useful is the posthumous third volume of Vernon L. Parrington's *Main Currents in American Thought* (New York, 1930). The development of an urban society that tremendously affected the transition in thought and attitude on the part of both government and the people, is best treated in Arthur M. Schlesinger, Sr., *The Rise of the City, 1878–1898* (New York, 1933) and Blake McKelvey, *The Urbanization of America, 1860–1915* (New Brunswick, 1963). For the development of the rural towns during this period, see the perceptive study of Lewis Atherton, *Main Street on the Middle Border* (Bloomington, 1954).

The literature on the origins and consequences of the Spanish-American War is voluminous, to put it mildly. The most useful starting point for an analysis of the events is still Julius W. Pratt, *Expansionists Of 1898*. H. Wayne Morgan's *America's Road to Empire: The War With Spain and Overseas Expansion* (New York, 1965), is a more updated study that is very critical of Ernest May, while downplaying the economic interpretations of Williams, LaFeber, et al. An older, but still useful, work is French Ensor Chadwick, *Relations of the United States and Spain: Diplomacy* (New York, 1909), while John L. Offner's unpublished work "President McKinley and the Origins of the Spanish-American War" (Ph.D. dissertation, Pennsylvania State University, 1957), throws much new light on America's "road to war" in 1898.

Paul S. Holbo has examined the nuances of Presidential political maneuvering in the weeks before the outbreak of war in "Presidential Leadership in Foreign Affairs: William McKinley and the Turpie-Foraker Amendment," *American Historical Review,* LXXII (July, 1967), pp. 1321–1335. The Spanish point of view on the advent of war with the United States is best represented in Jerónimo Becker, *Historia de las relaciones exteriores de España durante el siglo XIX* (3 vols., Madrid, 1924–1926), while the Cuban role in the struggle is ably argued by Herminio Portell Vila, *Historia de Cuba en sus relaciones can los Estados Unidos* (4 vols., Havana, 1938), and Emilio Roig de Leuchsenring, *Cuba y los Estados Unidos, 1805–1898* (Havana, 1949). For the Filipino background, see Teodoro A. Agoncillo, *Malolos: The Crisis of the Republic* (Quezon City, 1960), and the unpublished work of John N. Schumacher, S.J., "The Filipino Nationalists' Propaganda Campaign in Europe, 1880–1895" (Ph.D. dissertation, Georgetown University, 1965).

The role of public opinion in "forcing" war upon the McKinley Administration is most stridently argued in Joseph E. Wisan, *The Cuban Crisis as Reflected in the New York Press, 1895–1898* (New York, 1934) and Marcus M. Wilkerson, *Public Opinion and the Spanish-American War* (Baton Rouge, 1932). Contrary or modifying opinions can be found in the following: Thomas A. Bailey, *The Man in The Street: The Impact of American Public Opinion on Foreign Policy* (New York, 1948); William E. Leuchtenburg, "The Needless War With Spain" in Allan Nevins (ed.), *Times of Trial* (New York, 1958), pp. 177–196; George W. Auxier, "Middle Western Newspapers and the Spanish-American War, 1895–1898," *Mississippi Valley Historical Review,* XXVI (March, 1940), pp. 523–534; and Ray A. Billington, "The Origins of Middle Western Isolation," *Political Science Quarterly,* LX (March, 1945), pp. 44–64. The role of the press during the war is best treated in Charles H. Brown, *The Correspondents' War* (New York, 1967).

The best single volume on the actual conduct of hostilities is still the debunking survey by Walter Millis, *The Martial Spirit* (Cambridge, 1931). A briefer, updated version is Frank Freidel's *The Splendid Little War* (Boston, 1958). The most detailed account of the Cuban campaign is Herbert H. Sargent, *The Campaign of Santiago de Cuba* (3 vols., Chicago, 1907). The best overall account of naval operations is still French Ensor Chadwick, *The Relations of The United States and Spain: The Spanish-American War* (2 vols., New York, 1911), but see also Harold and Margaret Sprout, *The Rise of American Naval*

Power, 1776–1918 (Princeton, 1939) and the work of Braisted cited above. Dewey's conduct at Manila vis-à-vis the Germans in the weeks following his victory are best assessed in Thomas A. Bailey, "Dewey and the Germans At Manila Bay," *American Historical Review,* XLV (October, 1939), pp. 59–81. A useful supplement is Lester B. Shippee, "Germany and the Spanish-American War," *American Historical Review,* XXX (July, 1925), pp. 754–777. For varying accounts of the Filipino campaign, see Uldarico S. Baclagon, *Philippine Campaigns* (Manila, 1952), and James A. Le Roy, *The Americans in the Philippines* (2 vols., Boston, 1914). A searing indictment of American military operations in the Philippines is Leon Wolff's *Little Brown Brother* (Garden City, New York, 1961). Among the memoir accounts of the war, the most important are those of Frederick Funston, *Memoirs Of Two Wars: Cuban and Philippine Experiences* (New York, 1914), Emilio Aguinaldo y Famy, *A Second Look at America* (New York, 1957), and the relevant portions of the autobiographies of *George Dewey* (New York, 1913) and *Theodore Roosevelt* (New York, 1913). The war as viewed by a front-line soldier is perceptively analyzed in the diary account of Charles Johnson Post, *The Little War of Private Post* (Boston, 1960). A valuable insight into the conduct of the war itself by the McKinley Administration is Charles G. Dawes, *A Journal of the McKinley Years* (Chicago, 1950). For an analysis of American post-combat activities in the various war theatres, see Edward J. Berbusse, *The United States in Puerto Rico, 1898–1900* (Chapel Hill, 1966); David F. Healy, *The United States in Cuba, 1898–1902: Generals, Politicians And the Search for Policy* (Madison, 1963); Garel A. Grunder and William E. Livezey, *The Philippines and the United States* (Norman, Okla., 1951); and Earl S. Pomeroy, *Pacific Outpost: American Strategy in Guam and Micronesia* (Stanford, 1951). The best overview of the entire subject is still Julius W. Pratt, *America's Colonial Experiment: How the United States Gained, Governed, and in Part Gave Away a Colonial Empire* (New York, 1950).

The expansionist debate erupted in Congress and throughout the nation long before the cessation of hostilities. To date there is no published account of the armistice and peace negotiations, but see Richard H. Miller, "The Peace of Paris, 1898: A Case Study of the Dilemmas of Imperialism," (Ph.D. dissertation, Georgetown University, 1969). Miller argues that the decision to "go imperial" in the Caribbean and the Pacific antedated the war with Spain, and was finalized within a week after Dewey's victory at Manila. H. Wayne Morgan has performed a useful service in editing and publishing *Making*

Peace With Spain (Austin, 1965), Whitelaw Reid's diary of the negotiations at Paris.

The background history of Hawaiian annexation has been ably
treated in the works of R. S. Kuykendall, *The Hawaiian Kingdom,
1778–1893* (3 vols., Honolulu, 1938–1967); William A. Russ, Jr., *The
Hawaiian Republic (1894–1898), Its Struggle to Win Annexation* (Selins-
grove, Pa., 1961); Sylvester K. Stevens, *American Expansion in Hawaii,
1852–1898* (Harrisburg, 1945); and Merze Tate, *The United States and
the Hawaiian Kingdom* (New Haven, 1965). The Japanese role has
been fully developed in Hilary Conroy, *The Japanese Frontier in
Hawaii, 1868–1898* (Berkeley, 1953). Additional useful information on
the subject can be found in George W. Baker, "Benjamin Harrison and
Hawaiian Annexation: A Reinterpretation," *Pacific Historical Review,*
XXXIII (August, 1964), pp. 295–309; and two articles by Thomas A.
Bailey, viz., "Japan's Protest Against the Annexation of Hawaii,"
Journal of Modern History, III (March, 1931), pp. 46–61, and "The
United States and Hawaii During the Spanish-American War," *Ameri-
can Historical Review,* XXXVI (April, 1931), pp. 552–560. With re-
gard to the decision to annex the Philippines, in addition to the works
of Morgan, May, Miller, Agoncillo, and Pratt cited above, see also the
following articles: Thomas J. McCormick, "Insular Imperialism and
the Open Door: The China Market and the Spanish-American War,"
Pacific Historical Review, XXXII (May, 1963), pp. 155–169; and
James K. Eyre, Jr., "Japan and the American Annexation of the Philippines," *Pacific Historical Review,* XI (March, 1942), pp. 55–71 and
"Russia and the American Acquisition of the Philippines," *Mississippi
Valley Historical Review,* XXVIII (March, 1942), pp. 539–562.

The antiexpansionist response inspired by the events of 1898 has
captured the fancy of many historians in recent years. The best general introduction is still Fred H. Harrington, "The Anti-Imperialist
Movement in the United States, 1898–1900," *Mississippi Valley Historical Review,* XXII (September, 1935), pp. 211–230, which should be
supplemented by his "Literary Aspects of American Anti-Imperialism,"
New England Quarterly, X (December, 1937), pp. 650–667. The orthodox view on the subject is most cogently presented in Richard Hofstadter's revised essay, "Cuba, the Philippines and Manifest Destiny"
in *The Paranoid Style in American Politics and Other Essays* (New
York, 1965), pp. 145–187. A good background study to the anti-imperialist movement before 1898 is Donald M. Dozer's "Anti-Imperialism in
the United States, 1865–1895: Opposition to Annexation of Overseas
Territories" (Ph.D. dissertation, Harvard University, 1936). More

suggestive but limited in scope is Robert L. Beisner, *Twelve Against Empire: The Anti-Imperialists, 1898–1900* (New York, 1968). For a perceptive analysis of the role that racism played in both the imperial and anti-imperial arguments, see Christopher Lasch, "The Anti-Imperialists, the Philippines and the Inequality of Man," *Journal of Southern History*, XXIV (August, 1958), pp. 319–331. A similar approach is presented in Harold Baron, "Anti-Imperialism and the Democrats," *Science and Society*, XXI (Summer, 1958), pp. 222–239; and Maria C. Lanzar, "The Anti-Imperialist League," *Philippine Social Science Review*, III (August–November, 1930), pp. 7–41 and 118–132. The newly emerging Socialist Party in the United States was torn between humanitarianism and hysteria on the issue. For an able synopsis of their party conflicts over this problem, see Howard H. Quint, "American Socialists and the Spanish-American War," *American Quarterly*, X (1958), pp. 131–141.

Of the personalities involved in the expansionist debate, the most controversial is certainly William Jennings Bryan. The older interpretation of Bryan's role was best summarized in W. Stull Holt's *Treaties Defeated By The Senate: A Study of the Struggle Between President and Senate Over the Conduct of Foreign Relations* (Baltimore, 1933), but it has been completely undermined by the researches of Paolo E. Coletta and Richard H. Miller. In addition to his biography cited below, Coletta has put Bryan's activities in 1898 in their proper perspective in the following articles: "Bryan, McKinley And The Treaty Of Paris," *Pacific Historical Review*, XXVI (May, 1957), pp. 131–146; "McKinley, The Peace Negotiations and the Acquisition of the Philippines," *Pacific Historical Review*, XXX (November, 1961), pp. 341–350; and "Bryan, Anti-Imperialism and Missionary Diplomacy," *Nebraska History*, XLIV (September, 1963), pp. 167–187. Miller (see above) argues that McKinley and the Big Four (Senators Aldrich, Allison, Orville Platt, and Spooner) were much more influential in mustering support for the treaty than Bryan; in fact, he takes issue with Coletta in questioning whether Bryan influenced even a single Senate vote on the treaty. Though somewhat dated, Merle Curti's *Bryan and World Peace* (Northampton, Mass., 1931) offers a useful overview of Bryan's long career in pacifism. There is much work to be done in studying the Republican opposition to expansion; a good start has been made by Richard E. Welch, Jr. in "Senator George Frisbie Hoar and the Defeat of Anti-Imperialism, 1898–1900," *The Historian*, XXVI (May, 1964), pp. 362–380; and "Opponents and Colleagues: George Frisbie Hoar and Henry Cabot Lodge, 1898–1904," *New England*

Quarterly, XXXIX (June, 1966) , pp. 182–209.

The postwar effects of the imperialist debate on American foreign policy and partisan politics are provocatively summarized in the following articles: William E. Leuchtenburg, "Progressivism and Imperialism: The Progressive Movement and American Foreign Policy, 1898–1916," *Mississippi Valley Historical Review*, XXXIX (December, 1952), pp. 483–504; Padriac C. Kennedy, "La Follette's Imperialist Flirtation," *Pacific Historical Review*, XXIX (May, 1960) , pp. 131–144; John T. Farrell, "Background of the 1902 Taft Mission to Rome," *American Catholic Historical Review*, XXXVI (April, 1950) , pp. 1–32; Thomas A. Bailey, "Was the Presidential Election of 1900 a Mandate on Imperialism?," *Mississippi Valley Historical Review*, XXIV (June, 1937), pp. 43–52; and John W. Rollins, "The Anti-Imperialists and Twentieth Century American Foreign Policy," *Studies on the Left*, III (1962) , pp. 9–24. However, much work remains to be done in this area before one can render any definitive value judgments on the subject.

The historiographical controversy surrounding the Open Door policy properly belongs in a separate study, since this writer subscribes to the view first presented by Tyler Dennett (see above) that such a policy was operative long before the promotional campaign launched by John Hay in 1899. Recent scholarship has all but destroyed the arguments put forth at an earlier date by A. Whitney Griswold in *The Far Eastern Policy of the United States* (New Haven, 1938) and perpetuated by later writers such as George F. Kennan in *American Diplomacy, 1900–1950* (Chicago, 1951) and almost every textbook author on American history. Charles S. Campbell, Jr. paved the way for such revision in *Special Business Interests and the Open Door Policy* (New Haven, 1951) , while William R. Braisted added additional valuable information in "The United States and the China Development Company," *Far Eastern Quarterly*, XI (February, 1953) , pp. 147–165. In the decade of the sixties the final nails were driven into this historiographical coffin by two Americans, an Englishman, and an Australian. Thomas J. McCormick in *China Market: America's Quest for Informal Empire, 1893–1901* (Chicago, 1967) and Marilyn Blatt Young in *The Rhetoric of Empire: American China Policy, 1895–1901* (Cambridge, 1968) both accentuated the continuity of the China policy before and after the events of 1898, though differing slightly in their interpretation of the impact of Philippine annexation. J. A. S. Grenville's *Lord Salisbury and Foreign Policy: The Close of the Nineteenth Century* (London, 1964) and R. G. Neale's *Great Britain and United States Expansion: 1898–1900* (East Lansing, Mich., 1966) both play down the propagandizing efforts of Sir Charles Beresford, while reducing the significance of the roles of A. E. Hippesley and W. W. Rockhill as the dual inspiration for Hay's Open Door notes of 1899 and 1900. These findings have been incorporated into the latest synthesis on Anglo-American relations, Bradford Perkins' *The Great Rapprochement: England and the United States, 1895–1914* (New York, 1968), which tends to make earlier works obsolescent. However, Charles S. Campbell, Jr.'s *Anglo-American Understanding*, 1898–1903 (Baltimore, 1957) and A. E. Campbell's *Great Britain and the United States, 1895–1903* (London, 1960) are still useful, though both (and Perkins, too) should be used with caution in examining the British role in the Spanish-American war.

In the realm of biography, much work still remains to be done. Harry J. Sievers, *Benjamin Harrison* (3 vols., Chicago, New York and Indianapolis, 1952–1968), is the best on that president, but it is little more than an interim judgment on Harrison's handling of foreign policy. Allan Nevins' Pulitzer Prize biography, *Grover Cleveland: A Study in Courage* (New York, 1932), has mesmerized scholars for too long; a tentative first revisionist step in reducing his dimensions is Horace S. Merrill, *Bourbon Leader: Grover Cleveland and the Democratic Party* (Boston, 1957). Both leave much to be desired in their analyses of foreign policy; the reader would derive greater benefit by referring to the works of LaFeber and Grenville cited above. William McKinley has undergone a deserved historical rehabilitation in recent years, especially in Margaret Leech's *In the Days of McKinley* (New York, 1959) and H. Wayne Morgan's *William McKinley and His America* (Syracuse, 1963).

Theodore Roosevelt has attracted more attention from historians than his three predecessors combined. Among the superabundance of biographies available, the best for analyzing his foreign policy attitudes are Howard K. Beale, *Theodore Roosevelt and the Rise of America to World Power* (Baltimore, 1956), though his treatment of Roosevelt in the period 1894–1898 is the weakest in the book; Henry F. Pringle, *Theodore Roosevelt* (rev. ed., New York, 1956); and William H. Harbaugh, *Power and Responsibility: The Life and Times of Theodore Roosevelt* (New York, 1961). Two provocative shorter studies are John M. Blum, *The Republican Roosevelt* (Cambridge, 1954); and G. Wallace Chessman, *Theodore Roosevelt and the Politics of Power* (Boston, 1969). The reader should also consult the first volume of Henry F. Pringle, *The Life and Times of William Howard Taft* (2 vols., New York, 1939), for a better understanding of the evolution of American policy in the Philippines after 1898.

The general criticisms noted above apply even more trenchantly to the available studies on the secretaries of state during this period. Most of the earlier volumes in Samuel F. Bemis (ed.), *The American Secretaries of State and Their Diplomacy* (10 vols., New York, 1927–1929) are bland, pedestrian surveys that have been rendered obsolete by recent scholarship. The best study on Thomas F. Bayard is still Charles C. Tansill, *The Foreign Policy of Thomas F. Bayard* (New York, 1940); Alice Felt Tyler's *The Foreign Policy of James G. Blaine* (Minneapolis, 1927), though adequate, needs updating. There are no decent studies of Richard Olney (he deserves one), John Sherman, or William R. Day, but Tyler Dennett's *John Hay: From Poetry to Politics* (New York, 1934) is a very good starting point for a very complex man. Though Elihu Root did not become Secretary of State until 1905, he was an important policy figure in 1898–1899, especially after he replaced Russell A. Alger as Secretary of War. The best biographies of him thus far are Philip C. Jessup, *Elihu Root* (2 vols., New York, 1938) and Richard W. Leopold, *Elihu Root and the Conservative Tradition,* (Boston, 1954).

Among the available Congressional biographies, the most useful introductions to the period are John A. Garraty, *Henry Cabot Lodge* (New York, 1953), and Elmer Ellis, *Henry Moore Teller, Defender Of The West* (Caldwell, Idaho, 1941). The Big Four of the Senate have been less than well treated to date; the most adequate studies thus far are Nathaniel W. Stephenson, *Nelson W. Aldrich: A Leader in American Politics* (New York, 1930); Leland L. Sage, *William Boyd Allison: A Study in Practical Politics* (Iowa City, 1956); and Dorothy G. Fowler, *John Coit Spooner, Defender of Presidents* (New York, 1961). Orville Platt, the other member of the quartet, has yet to find even an adequate chronicler. Thomas Beer's *Hanna* (New York, 1929) and William A. Robinson's *Thomas B. Reed, Parliamentarian* (New York, 1930) only scratch the surface of two of the most important—and intriguing—men of the period. Other Congressional biographies of relative importance are Frederick H. Gillett, *George Frisbie Hoar* (Boston, 1934); John R. Lambert, *Arthur Pue Gorman* (Baton Rouge, 1953); and Edward L. Younger, *John A. Kasson: Politics and Diplomacy from Lincoln to McKinley* (Iowa City, 1955). In many respects, the most important political biography of the period is Paolo E. Coletta's *William Jennings Bryan* (3 vols., Lincoln, 1964–1969), which far transcends anything else done on the man or the movements with which he was associated.

Unfortunately, there is virtually nothing in the field of military biography for this period, but the interested student ought to read the initial chapters of Elting E. Morison's *Admiral Sims and the Modern American Navy* (Boston, 1942), for the intriguing role played in the Spanish-American War by the man who was the most important American sailor in World War I. Other significant biographies that throw additional light on the events of the time are W. A. Swanberg's *Citizen Hearst* (New York, 1961), and *Pulitzer* (New York, 1967); James H. Moynihan, *The Life of Archbishop John Ireland* (New York, 1953), which details Ireland's important role as an intermediary between the Papacy and McKinley; Burton J. Hendrick, *The Life of Andrew Carnegie* (2 vols., Garden City, New York, 1932); Edward C. Kirkland's masterful *Charles Francis Adams, Jr., 1835–1915: The Patrician at Bay* (Cambridge, 1965); and Paul A. Varg, *Open Door Diplomat: The Life of W. W. Rockhill* (Urbana, 1952).

Finally, if the reader's lust for information on this period has not been satiated by the works cited above, or the reference bibliographies contained therein, he is referred to the following additional bibliographical tools: Samuel F. Bemis and Grace G. Griffin (eds.), *Guide to the Diplomatic History of the United States, 1775–1921* (Washington, 1935); Council on Foreign Relations, *Foreign Affairs Bibliography* (4 vols., New York, 1933–1964); G. F. Howe et al. (eds.), *The American Historical Association's Guide to Historical Literature* (Washington, 1960–   ); Oscar Handlin et al. (eds.), *Harvard Guide to American History* (rev. ed., Cambridge, 1960); and David F. Trask et al. (eds.), *A Bibliography of United States–Latin American Relations Since 1810* (Lincoln, 1969). If this is not sufficient, then this writer can only suggest the card catalogue of the Library of Congress—or a new subject for study.